THE HIDDEN WEALTH OF TANZANIA

Martin P. Mandalu, PhD

Stella Maris Mtwara University College

Printed by CreateSpace
An Amazon.com Company

The Hidden Wealth of Tanzania

© 2017 Martin P. Mandalu
mpmandalu@gmail.com

ISBN-13: 978-1978203280

ISBN-10: 1978203284

RECOMMENDED CITATION

Mandalu, M.P. 2017. *The Hidden Wealth of Tanzania.*
Columbia, SC: CreateSpace.

Available at
https://www.amazon.com/Hidden-Wealth-Tanzania-Martin-
Mandalu/dp/1978203284

Acknowledgments

We human beings are a summation of all we acquire from those who teach us directly and/or indirectly. I am grateful to a large number of individuals who made it possible for the realisation of this book. Some provided a critical and intellectual assistance, others offered time to listen to raw ideas and others assisted with the financial resources.

Mr Robert Stephen Bundala bore the pain of going through the whole manuscript several times. I am indeed indebted to him for his insightful input and for the editing work that he put in with lots of love. I acknowledge the critical input from Mr Nelson Chrysostom Lupogo who, through our many discussions, insisted on some matters to be put in the right presentation style that would stimulate the reader's mind. I am equally thankful to Professor Thakhathi, D.R and Professor Hofisi Costa, my PhD sponsors, who journeyed with me in the course of my doctorate studies; the experience which provide the backbone to this book. I sincerely appreciate many researchers whose works informed my humble thoughts to generate this book. The scholars before me are truly giants that shoulder us all to see beyond the horizon. The list of references is a sign of my gratitude to you all.

I am deeply indebted to my family. My wife Namangi and our sons, Alexander and Aaron, deserve special credit for allowing me to concentrate on this work at the time that was rightly theirs. Their patience, encouragement and support were vital for me to realise this oeuvre and thus be able to present to you this food for thought for the betterment of our people and the society.

As I acknowledge the contribution and input from a litany of friends; I appreciate all their valuable input and do share with them all the strength found in the book. However, I am accountable and responsible for all shortcomings in the book.

Dedication

For Namangi, Alexander and Aaron

Foreword

In the book Dr. Mandalu takes us back to a recent past of Tanzania, then Tanganyika, to demonstrate the strength and patriotism of the dwellers of this land. Through Ntemi Mirambo and Mtwa Mkwawa, he exhibits the courage, intelligence, cooperation and other qualities of the Tanzanian people. He demonstrates as well how those attributes were destroyed during colonialism before being restored through independence and self-determination.

In the economic history of an independent Tanzania, the author takes us through the whole economic trajectory taken by Tanzania since independence; right through the relatively short period of Market economy, Ujamaa period, which marked the economy and its people significantly, and up until the neo-liberal age that appears to be influencing the country's thinking today.

The economic epochs experimented in the country were well accompanied by economic development theories that were employed directly or indirectly by the state. Systematically, the author illustrates the success and limitations of modernization, dependency and neoliberal thinking. Modernization defined the brief market economy immediately after independence, whereas the dependency period informed the Ujamaa ideology and neo-liberalism informs the capitalist thinking.

The book reminds us that when the Ujamaa practices did not match with the plans, interior and exterior forces obliged the state go into neoliberalism which at that time was perceived to be the saviour of the economy. However, neo-liberalism- the messiah, failed to save the day. Thus the search for the remedy continues as the state cannot and should not exist without identity.

In transition for the right remedy to address peoples' development, the author reveals that Tanzania is neither socialist nor capitalist. The fact that the country lacks a defined ideology makes it difficult to be predictable and thus, to some extent, hinders the private sector from flourishing and thus limiting human development.

In the search for an ideology, Dr. Martin Mandalu presents a number of models from which Tanzania can gain experience and learn. The author demonstrates to readers that developmental state is the right model for Tanzania to tailor its own. Moreover, he proposes pragmatic action for a successful developmental state in case the state subscribes to the former.

Finally the book concludes with a call for a total transformation of people's thinking for development. The author argues that the true wealth of this nation is hidden and buried deep in each individual's brain and thoughts. It is hidden in their ability to think correctly and transform their ideas into pragmatic innovations to improve life.

Dar es Salaam,
Dr. Slaus Titus Mwisomba

Preface

In the book I discuss issues known so well by most senior citizens in the country but seem to be forgotten despite their importance. Some part of the book is informed by a rigorous literature review and data collected in field work that were employed in a PhD thesis entitled Tanzania's Development Agenda and Poverty Reduction: A case of MKUKUTA I. The current volume which has a different theme adopts and adapts some thinking from the mentioned research. The book intends to contribute in the fields of development studies and philosophy by employing an approach that is either new or simply ignored by development stakeholders. The approach is discussed throughout the book but reaches its peak in chapter eight of the book "The Hidden Wealth of Tanzania".

The Hidden Wealth of Tanzania is the chapter that carries the title of the book. It introduces an unholy trinity, a relatively new approach to development, which aims at provoking discussion and debates on how our future entrepreneurs, business owners and public servants should be prepared if at all we wish, as one people, to industrialise and be innovative while contributing significantly to the world. The proposed approach discusses how we can benefit from the many hidden talents and potentials. It argues that our people are capable of identifying and using their God given talents to benefit societies sustainably while preserving resources for the future generations.

The other themes discussed in the book include, but not limited to, the following:

- o Tanzania is neither socialist nor capitalist! What ideology does it carry on the road to industrialisation?
- o Some scholars in Tanzania were trained under pure capitalism. However Mwalimu Nyerere made them members of his cabinet to work under the Ujamaa ideology. Did that contribute to the failure of Ujamaa?
- o On villagisation the rural dwellers were not well educated on the significance of the same hence resistance. Are rural people, the majority in the country, well informed about industrialisation today?
- o Is Western democracy necessary for industrialisation? Why is it that some countries are prospering without the same?
- o Is the international community necessary for economic development of the under developed states?

o   Which Eastern model should African states employ for industrialization? Should it be the Malaysian or South Korean model?

o   What can the current leaders learn from ancient ones such as Mirambo and Mkwawa?

o   How do scholars, in least developed countries, play part in economic development?

o   How can today's students contribute to their country's economic development?

o   How does the mass media participate in the country's development agenda?

o   Is Rwanda the role model for development in Africa?

CONTENTS

CHAPTER ONE

THE BEGINNING OF A NATION

"Man[1] is a political animal" so claimed Aristotle in his "Politics". Tanzanians are members of that kingdom with highly developed brains and gifted intelligence that distinguishes him from other members in the kingdom. Therefore, it follows logically that Tanzanians are political and intelligent animals.

Political animals, through social contract, organize themselves as they look for ways of self-governing. Through self-governance, the people decide on who gets what, when, how and why they should get it and at a particular time[2]. Depending on institutions and leadership in a state; in many cases the wish is one thing and the practice is completely different from the theory. Governance in a state at times does not at all relate to the leadership theories in a particular country;

---

[1] Man in this book refers to human beings for both man (he) and woman (she) and this will be used throughout in the book to mean that unless stated otherwise.
[2] Politics: Who Gets What, When, How by Harold Lasswell (1957/58)

but all the same, no matter how weak local leaders could be, self-governance should always be preferred to colonialism.

Modern Tanzania[3] is a state comprised of a number of tribes (over 120). These tribes used to be "small nations" occupying large land space, some as large as 200,000 km^2 and even more for large ones such as the Sukuma, Haya, Nyakyusa, Chagga, Zaramo, Nyamwezi[4] and so on. The territory sizes that they occupied could be the same size or even larger than some small European countries such as Montenegro (13,812 km^2), Kosovo (10,887 km^2), Cyprus (9,251km^2), Luxembourg (2,586 km^2), Monaco (1.95 km^2) Andorra (468 km^2) and others[5].

---

[3] Tanzania is a united republic composed of two independent states namely Tanganyika and Zanzibar. Tanganyika became independent on 09th December 1961 and Zanzibar on 12th December 1963. The two states: (Tanganyika + Zanzibar) united on 26th April 1964 to become Tanzania

[4] The author of the article about Mirambo claimed that the territory that he (Mirambo) governed was as large as 200,000km^2
https://afrolegends.com/2014/05/05/mirambo-the-black-napoleon/

[5] .https://www.skyscanner.net/news/europe-s-10-smallest-countries-where-small-beautiful accessed on 20/10/2016

A score of African countries experienced civil wars of which some were instigated by tribalism[6]. Such wars claimed large number of innocent lives and resources. Some of the civil wars lasted for decades and left deep wounds in the countries. However, Tanzania was spared by such wars as people of all tribes in the country have friendly relationships and can freely move and carry out their social, political and economic activities anywhere in the country. This calls for much thanks to the strong leadership of the founding leaders and God's grace that people are conscious of their tribes but unconscious of tribal divisions. The work of the founding leaders of this great nation such as Julius Nyerere, Abeid Karume, Titi Mohamed, Kingunge Ngobale Mwiru, Rashid Kawawa[7], and many others, was indeed fundamental for the peace and tranquility that the people of Tanzania enjoy today. It is important to note that things have not always been like that.

---

[6] A tribe is that of which nobody chooses to have but rather they are born into thanks to the choices of partners made by offspring's parents. Tribes are good as they are a source of values, norms and customs. However, nobody should claim his tribe to be superior to others— it is true that tribes are different and it is important for them to be different for they enrich a nation through inherited values since ages. However, it is important to keep this in mind that *no tribe is superior to the other; they are just different.*

[7] Consult the list of the founding members of TANU in 1954 and those of TAA

In the past, tribes used to have rivalry and indeed hostile relationship with neighbouring nations and foreign invaders. However, the people were keen and patriotic enough to protect their land. Population is one of the components of a state. In the old nations, people, though had weak weapons, still fought for their land, values and respect as a people. Thus countries are indeed made up of patriotic citizens. When people are really patriotic, they are ready to fight and even die for their countries. However, the moment that a number of tribes find themselves in one state; one large territory, they should then come together to form a united country out of many nations (tribes) as did the Tanzanians[8].

I will share with you a case of two tribal leaders to demonstrate how those nations through their leaders were proud of their states, traditions, and cultures and were ready to defend their territories; even sacrificing their own life. Tanzania is formed out of many tribes that were proud of their traditions and were ready to

---

[88] In the territory of Tanganyika and now Tanzania there were many tribes (nations) in the same state, following good leadership and God's grace they have been able to live together peaceful

defend them. Nevertheless when those tribes found themselves in the today's territory of Tanzania, they peacefully agreed to form one country respecting each other despite their differences. The unity, equality and amicable relationship amongst tribes in Tanzania can be witnessed and justified through the uncountable intermarriages, socio-economic activities, and free movement practiced and experienced by people of all ethnic groups, religions and political ideologies in the country.

The case of Mkwawa

The Hehe nation became popular through their most prominent and historical leader, Mkwawa, who was one of the sons of Munyigumba[9]. However, it is Munyigumba who is believed to have died in 1878/79, that was the first chief (Mtwa) who united the Hehe as a strong people. He was the Mtwa of the Ng'uluhe chiefdom which lie at the centre of modern Uhehe and was under the Muyinga dynasty (Redmayne, 1968). Munyigumba managed to assert his authority over all the surrounding chiefdoms. However, it is not known

---

[9] Some sons of Munyigumba included Muhenga, Mkwawa, Mulimbila, Mpangile

5

exactly what tactics he used to manage his nation. At the international platform, that is in relation to other proximate tribes, Munyigumba had not been militarily successful against immediate tribes that had acquired military recognition earlier than the Hehe. The tribes in question included the Bena, the Sangu and the Ngoni. However, before his death he had won major battles against each of those people and ruled a much larger territory than other nearby chiefs (ibid).

Mkwawa, who was born in 1855 at Luhota, was one of the sons of Mtwa Munyigumba. Mkwawa and his brother Muhenga were in the succession plan of their father. Munyigumba had willed that his expanded territory should be divided into two and ruled by his sons after his death. However, Mwambabe the son-in-law of Munyigumba who was of Nyamwezi origin took over power after the death of Munyigumba. Mwambabe was assisted by Muhenga to take over power as an attempt for Muhenga himself to rule in the throne of his father. Sensing danger Mkwawa fled to Ugogo[10].

---

[10] Redmayne, Alison. (1968) in Mkwawa and the Hehe Wars and
http://www.mkwawa.com

From this narration there are interesting phenomena that relate to modern Tanzania. Mwambabe, who was Nyamwezi by tribe, married one of the daughters of the chief from another nation. This relates to what we experience in modern Tanzania. There are intermarriages among almost all tribes. When Mkwawa sensed danger he went into exile in Ugogo seeking for asylum in another country. In our modern world what Mkwawa did is not uncommon. We experience people leaving their countries for safety in other countries.

When in Ugogo, Mkwawa was persuaded by his admirers and supporters to return to Uhehe. He came back and consolidated his strength at Kalenga. From there he fought Mwambabe at a place that came to be known as Ilundamatwe[11] and took over the chiefdom. During his reign as Mtwa of the Hehe, no chiefs were able to defeat Mtwa Mkwawa. Owing to that he kept on expanding his territory far beyond borders that were left by his late father, Mtwa Munyigumba, through winning wars.

---

[11] A place where there is a heap of heads, that is demonstrating the fierce battle that was fought

During his reign Mkwawa fought and won many battles. Consequently the Hehe became known as warmongers. Though we are told that Mtwa Mkwawa was a merciless leader; a no nonsense one (Redmayne, 1968), he was well organised during his reign. He battled and emerged victorious in many wars for the purpose of expanding his territory. When the Germans came to East Africa in the 1800s, Mkwawa resisted their invasion and defeated them for a while. All this was in defence of his nation. Moreover, he fought any chiefdoms that allowed Germans' invasion. Consequently most surrounding nations feared him. As he expanded his territory he somehow followed, at least part of the just war theory, that is during war he did not kill those who surrendered. Instead he left them continue as chiefs in their chiefdoms so long as they acknowledged his supremacy.

Mkwawa and the Hehe became even more popular when the Hehe under the leadership of Mtwa Mkwawa defeated a Gernman expedition in a battle fought at Lugalo on 17th August 1891 and thereafter continued with resistance against the Germans' invasions for seven years, up to the time when Mkwawa decided to take his own life rather than being captured live by his enemies. The Hehe resistance against well-equipped German invaders was costly to both sides. Germans were astonished by the Hehe grit and their war strategies; as well as their competency, despite using relatively weak weapons as compared to Germans[12].

To rule as successfully as Mkwawa calls for special abilities. For the case of Mtwa Mkwawa, his qualities and abilities came from different sources; his ancestors, intelligence, talents and super natural powers to mention a few. Mkwawa's mother was seNgimba. She belonged to the Muyinga dynasty. Mkwawa believed in his departed ancestors to whom he was connected through prayers, sacrifices, and offerings. Through this practice he received strengths and supernatural power[13]. Moreover, Mkwawa's intelligence and expertise in a number of fields is witnessed in his success in the many wars fought and

---

[12] http://www.mkwawa.com/lugalo
[13] This is indeed in line to what Mbiti, Nyamiti and other African Philosophers argue that an African is always a religious person and that he practices religion throughout his entire life activities.

won, his wealth accumulation through trade, and ability to form allegiance and coalition.

Furthermore, Mtwa Mkwawa put accent on agriculture as a reliable means for food security to himself and his subjects. During grace periods he ordered his citizens to bring food to the palace at Kalenga for storage to be used during hostile seasons. However, during famine he organised for distribution of food supply to his subjects[14].

The case of Mirambo

Mirambo, born as Mbula Mtelya, was born in 1840. He inherited kingship (Ntemi) of the chiefdom on Uyowa from his father Ntemi Kasanda, a well-known warrior, in 1858. Mirambo united two chiefdoms located in western Tabora that were found in the kingdom of Unyanyembe[15].

Mirambo, through both of his parents, was a descendant of Mshimba who was the last king of a well-known

---

[14] http://www.mkwawa.com and Redmayne, 1968

[15] https://afrolegends.com/2014/05/05/mirambo-the-black-napoleon/

- http://www.blackpast.org/gah/mirambo-ca-1840-1884 Accessed on 09/08/2017

kingdom of Usagali. Thus Mirambo intended to rebuild the old kingdom. In 1860, Mirambo built a new Nyamwezi state; the Urambo from Mirambo. Mirambo was the name he had picked for himself meaning corpses in his mother tongue. He built his capital at Iseramagazi; a fortified residence built of dry bricks which were well decorated.

Ntemi Mirambo united the Nyamwezi as a strong people and made it hard for invaders to conquer the region easily. While he made it hard for invaders and European explorers' penetration, much earlier he had taken control over the Swahili-Arab trade route imposing tax for the caravans that crossed his territory.

Mirambo knew the strength of the Ngoni in war and so he learned their language and their military skills. He later strengthened the performance of his army which he named as the Ngoni did, rugaruga. In 1860, he conquered a nearby chiefdom of Ulyankuru. Since then Mirambo was busy expanding and strengthening his territory. He expanded his territory along the banks of River Gombe giving hard time to Arab traders[16].

In 1871 he defeated the Arab traders nearby Tabora. Mirambo's resistance was extraordinary for the Nyamwezi rugaruga were so patriotic that they would go to the extent of melting their copper jewels to make ammunitions for their guns. Every year Mirambo had expansion plans and so he sent soldiers to different directions for the same purpose. By 1878, the territory in the North had expanded up to the southern banks of Lake Victoria and by 1881, in the west the expansion had gone nearby Uvinza for the control of Lake Tanganyika. Mirambo controlled caravans that passed in his territory and were obliged to pay levy for the passage.

Mirambo was perceived differently by different people. He was hated by the Arabs for disrupting their business that they had formerly controlled in the region. He was

[16] https://afrolegends.com/2014/05/05/mirambo-the-black-napoleon/
– http://www.blackpast.org/gah/mirambo-ca-1840-1884 Accessed on 09/08/2017

feared by the nearby kings, and for the Europeans he was truly a strong antagonist[17].

Mirambo practiced as well international politics as we know it today, though it should be understood from his period and context. Following his control of the Swahili – Arabs trade routes, he consequently disturbed the interests of the Buganda kingdom in the north which was under Kabaka Mutesa. The Buganda kingdom traded greatly with the Arabs and so Mutesa planned to attack Mirambo in the 1870s. Ntemi Mirambo was aware of the military strength of Kabaka Mutesa and so opted for diplomatic resolution by sending his ambassadors to Mutesa. Kabaka Mutesa reciprocated by sending his diplomatic corps to Urambo for peace talks. The two kings came to a consensus and formed a coalition in 1881[18]

---

[17] –https://afrolegends.com/2014/05/05/mirambo-the-black-napoleon/
–https://www.britannica.com/biography/Mirambo
–https://www.jamiiforums.com/threads/mirambo-the-man-who-changed-the-face-of-nineteenth-century-tanzania.424773/
[18]https://www.jamiiforums.com/threads/mirambo-the-man-who-changed-the-face-of-nineteenth-century-tanzania.424773/ Accessed on 09/08/2017
– http://www.blackpast.org/gah/mirambo-ca-1840-1884 Accessed on 09/08/2017

Mirambo was an organized, intelligent and simple man totally immersed in his culture and traditions. In his political system he allowed the chiefs he defeated in wars to continue ruling in their chiefdoms so long as they acknowledged his authority over them. In his capital which served for military and economic matters, Ntemi Mirambo was in charge of affairs. He regulated commodities' prices in the market and structured the consumption of alcohol.

Mirambo died on 2nd December 1844 after great accomplishments as one amongst great Ntemis of the Nyamwezi nation. In a nutshell, Mirambo could be described in four different perspectives. He was the traditional king, the warrior leader, the state builder and the modernizer.[19]

When strong traditional chiefs died the invaders had become too strong for the local kings to stop them from

---

[19]-https://www.jamiiforums.com/threads/mirambo-the-man-who-changed-the-face-of-nineteenth-century-tanzania.424773/ Accessed on 09/08/2017
- http://www.blackpast.org/gah/mirambo-ca-1840-1884 Accessed on 09/08/2017
-https://afrolegends.com/2014/05/05/mirambo-the-black-napoleon/
-https://www.britannica.com/biography/Mirambo accessed online 09/08/2017

invading. Ultimately Tanganyika fell in the hands of colonialists. The Germans took hold of Tanganyika as their territory in the 1880s.

Lessons from Mtwa Mkwawa and Ntemi Mirambo

We can pick a number of lessons from our traditional leaders who are our fore parents. From our parents we inherit our genetic make-up and some qualities and defects that define us. These two kings Mkwawa and Mirambo are representatives of early African society's leaders who had leadership qualities that can be passed on today for leadership. Some of the qualities demonstrated include patriotism, visionary spirit, grit, innovation, war strategies, economic consciousness, diplomacy and sovereignty, to mention a few.

In the narration of Mtwa Mkwawa we experience patriotism demonstrated evidently by that leader. Mkwawa defended his country against foreign invaders, rejecting imposition of foreign trade systems, and defending traditional values.

Moreover, the king introduced tax as one of the means to govern his country efficiently. Mtwa Mkwawa demanded his subjects to bring food staff to the palace and redistribute it to the population during famine. However the population was expected to cater for its own needs. Thus redistribution would only be exercised during complete starvation.

From circumstantial evidence, the two kings knew several languages which were learnt for a number of reasons. Mkwawa fled to Ugogo where he should have learnt some *Kigogo* to facilitate the asylum he was offered. Mirambo knew several languages for specific purposes. He wanted to learn military techniques from the Ngoni, so he learnt their language. He sent a diplomatic convoy to Buganda, though there could have been interpreters, there was a possibility that he knew some *Luganda*. Moreover, since he was in contact with the Arabs, it is possible that he had some Arabic language skills too, to facilitate tax collection.

Mirambo, just like Mkwawa, was a competent and patriotic leader. He protected his nation and expanded it through invading and conquering other kingdoms. Was he with capitalistic elements as he expanded his territory by colonising others? Moreover, he controlled economic matters in his territory as he regulated market prices, consumption of alcohol and collected tax from those who crossed his territory.

Tanzania under Foreign Powers[20]

Tanganyika became a colonial state when the African continent was divided amongst European countries in the Berlin conference in 1884. It was then that its history, economy and politics though of small nations such as those of Hehe under Mkwawa and Nyamwezi under Mirambo became officially known to Europeans. When the invaders succeeded at making Tanganyika their colony, that is appropriating a piece of land on the face of the earth for themselves, several tribes with their own wealth of values, traditions, economy, and politics were found under the same territory that is today known as Tanzania. Under colonialism Tanzania became totally transformed as it became integrated to international economy, civilization and politics; although

---

[20] The history of Tanzania can be traced back to as early as 1st and 2nd century AD, *http://www.our-africa.org/tanzania/history-politics*, however, the history taught at school does not give much details of our peoples' history; this calls for more research on the same. Let our history experts' work on that.

17

mainly at its disadvantage as the international incorporation benefited essentially the colonialists.

From the economic scope, Tanzania became a producer of crops which were mostly sold by colonialists to the international markets. Our farmers from several parts of the country produced a wide variety of crops some of which were cotton, tobacco, tea, cashew nut, ground nuts, and sisal. All these crops together with other natural productss were sold across the borders to benefit European countries. Tanganyika became a producer of raw materials to feed the European industries with what colonialists needed to run their industries. It is this phenomenon that several historians and African sympathisers wrote to remind Europeans on how they stripped Africa off of its wealth. Walter Rodney in his *How Europe Underdeveloped Africa* is one of the writers who clearly depict how the continent, Tanzania included, was stolen of its wealth.

On civilization, Tanzania was linked and introduced to the world through construction of some modern infrastructures such as railways as evidenced by the central railway from Dar es Salaam to Kigoma and Mwanza. The railway though built during colonial periods has been serving Tanzanians as a reliable source of transport. However, the Tanzanian government has significantly invested on modern roads to link all the regions. Though the rail construction was a great undertaking that linked Tanzania to the world, the railway aimed largely at serving the colonial interests. The railway transported crops from different parts of the country to the Dar es Salaam port for export to Europe. Indeed this is how Europe played part in underdeveloping the continent and Tanzania as Africans fed European industries with raw materials while Africa turned into a market of their own crops which were processed in Europe into high quality products. Past Europeans wrong doing to Africa does not mean Africans should continue mourning over the European theft but rather Africans need to think on how to improve the living standards of many of their people. This can be done by empowering the people with pragmatic education and thus giving them hope.

Moreover, it was during this colonial period that Tanzania was introduced to world politics. Tanzania was involved in world politics mostly through the First World War in 1914-1918 when it provided financial assistance and some Tanzanians were involved in the battle. The Tanzanian soldiers participated in the war not for the purpose of defending their country's interests but those of their colonial master- Germans by then. During the Second World War in 1939-1945 under the British: soldiers, wealth and other Tanzanian resources served in the war for the British interests. While the Tanzanian contribution to the two world wars was of great importance to their colonial masters, it also served to the Tanzanian welfare. We read in history books that it is thanks to the world wars that Africans' eyes and minds were opened to international politics and realised their rights for self-rule. The exposure they obtained through that encounter with people from different countries changed them forever.

During British colonialism in Tanganyika, some civil society organisations that served for the interests of few individuals of particular affiliations and professions started emerging. The civil society organisations were necessary because the British used the indirect rule system to govern the people. Africans were officially recognised as members of a tribe which was led by a certain chief. In such a system some chiefs became puppets of the British at the expense of their own tribe's men hence the need for other outlets that would address for people's needs even if under limited freedom and recognition by the colonial power.

However most of such organisations did not speak for the interests of all the people. There were efforts by some individuals to form organisations that would be more inclusive. It was under such circumstances that Tanganyika African Association (TAA) was born.

The TAA, which according to history was formed in 1920s for the purpose of uniting Africans to demand for their rights and meet their needs as they were marginalised by the indirect rule of the British, gave birth to a new political party. The Tanganyika African National Union (TANU) was born on July 7th 1954. TANU inherited from TAA experience and work strategies as it embarked on a much higher goal of demanding for independence for all people living in Tanganyika. TANU was so inclusive that it welcomed people of all races, religions, gender and any other differences to join hands and fight for independence and the rest now serves as part of history.

CHAPTER TWO

THE ECONOMY IN HISTORY

As we want to rediscover the hidden wealth in this beautiful country, Tanzania, I invite you to take a survey of her economic history which is indeed unique and fascinating. It is important to bear in mind that the following discussion concerns an independent Tanganyika and then Tanzania. In this book Tanzania is referred to as mainland Tanzania even though Tanzania, as stated earlier, is a united republic of Tanganyika and Zanzibar.

This chapter is dedicated to the economic history of Tanzania. However, I do not pretend to be covering all details of the economic history of this state. Nevertheless, you can be sure of getting important basics of the Tanzanian economy. The country has gone through three distinct periods that have shaped this East African state to be what it is today in all social, political, and economic spheres. The periods are the market economy, the Ujamaa and capitalistic periods.

The Market Economy (1961–1966)

When Tanzania, then Tanganyika, became independent in 1961, it inherited from the British colonialists a market economy (Ngowi, 2009; Boesen et al., 1977:14). However, the country was poor, and many parts of the country were dominated by subsistence economy which was predominately agricultural. Agriculture accounted for 59 percent of GDP in 1961, whereas the other sectors such as manufacturing produced only 3.6 percent and the rest which included transport, construction, mining, commerce, public utilities and services were reasonably small. The economy depended heavily on the agricultural sector which supported other minor sectors to produce survival output for the majority of the population (Silver, 1984 in Sansa 2010). Right from independence, the government agenda was to fight against poverty (Tanzania 2012:1–3). Ngowi (2009), contends that while the majority of the people were poor, the economy was in the hands of a few British colonial masters and Asian business people, specifically Arabs and Indians. The major means of economy which included industries, plantations, banks, mines and other major businesses were still in the ownership of the British and Asians, and this market economy was characterised by a capitalistic private sector. Todaro and Smith (2009), argue that when African countries became independent, their role model was the community of developed countries that had developed through capital accumulation and industrialisation which African countries could follow and industrialise as well. According to Kaiser (1996) in Ngowi (2009), immediately after independence, Tanzania followed an economic agenda that depended heavily on foreign investment to run a capital intensive industrialisation and agricultural development to attain its development goals.

Pratt (1976) in Sansa (2010), argues that the adoption of the market economy called for expansion of production through creation of employment opportunities in productive sectors and that end called for transformation of tribal subsistence into market

25

economy. To meet this objective, the government, through the Three-Year Development Plan 1961-1964, planned to expand the formal wage-earning activities by expanding the public services, industrial and agricultural activities and encouraged workers, through increased minimum wages, to settle permanently in towns. Rutman (1968) in Sansa (2010), reveals that the government, through the Three-Year Development Plan 1961-1964 and the First Five Year Development Plan of 1964/65-1968/69, envisaged rapid economic growth through stimulation of production in the two major productive sectors of agriculture and industry.

The IMF (1969) in Sansa (2010), indicates that by 1966, the real output was growing at 4.8 percent and 5.8 percent at current prices while the GDP grew at 6.7 percent yearly, as planned. The non-agricultural sector, especially manufacturing, which did not employ many people, continued to expand. The agriculture's contribution to GDP, which averaged 59 percent from 1961 to 1964, dropped to 54 percent in 1965 and declined further to 53 percent in 1966. The National income, at current prices, increased steadily from 1961 to 1966; except for the 1965 slowdown, the growth averaged 6.7 percent.

According to Silver (1984) in Sansa (2010), the manufacturing production continued to grow. It rose between 1960 and 1961 at a grand rate of 23 percent. Other industrial sectors experienced limited growth over the same period of time. The annual average growth rates for mining and quarrying was 0.2 percent, electricity and water recorded 4.5 percent and the construction industry 1.8 percent. Agriculture, which involved most common citizens, grew at 4.8 percent yearly from 1961 to 1965, whereas in the same period, transport grew at an average of 4.7 percent and commerce, rent and services at 5.2 percent. The rapid manufacturing output growth, as compared to other sectors, was reflected in the change of its contribution to GDP at current prices over the period. The proportion contribution of the manufacturing sub-sector to GDP in 1961 was at 3.6 percent and had increased impressively to 7.6 percent in 1965.

Therefore, the industrial sector, which involved few people and where manufacturing was a sub-sector, had grown very fast as compared to other sectors. In 1961, it recorded 10.1 percent and rose dramatically to 14.1 percent in 1965. However, Seidman (1972) in Sansa (2010), maintains that despite remarkable growth, particularly in the industry sector, this same period experienced market failure and slow growth output in the sisal sub-sector, resulting in poor performance in the agricultural processing sector. This led to a decline in employment in the sisal sub-sector and in the agriculture sector, as can be witnessed on the table below, this meant that ordinary citizens suffered the pain, and the government development agenda of poverty reduction was not being met. As it is witnessed on the table below, the percentage of people with agriculture as their source of income kept on increasing. This means that the number of poor people was increasing as agriculture's output, compared to the industry sector, kept on decreasing yearly.

Table 1: Total Employment in the Agricultural Sector 1962 – 1966

Sub-sectors	1962	1963	1964	1965	1966
Sisal	117,898	94,537	96, 396	76,493	64,593
Tea	19,239	14,900	13,882	11,757	12,106
Coffee	15,958	12,713	13,823	13,616	14,983
Sugar	8,704	8,275	8,442	8,739	8,758
Sub-Total	161,799	130,425	132,543	110,605	100,440
Agriculture	192,924	155,506	153,410	127,336	114,319
Percentage (%)	83.9	83.9	86.4	86.9	87.9

Source: Adapted from Sansa (2010) Table 5.6

Ngowi (2009), reiterates that the government had inherited colonial economic system of which it did not have the mandate to rectify economic problems when the market failed. Being a capitalistic economy, it entailed private ownership of major means of production and thus market forces drove the economy. In the mid-1960s a number of imbalances were experienced. This experience led to market failures. However, the government had no power to intervene over the market forces. The people's independence expectations were not met as they lived in more or less the same situation as before independence. They continued to labour for the same colonial masters they had worked for before independence.

29

In addition, the government development agenda of poverty reduction amongst the people was not being realised. Thus, as Kaiser (1996) argues in Ngowi (2009), the government realised that Ujamaa was the right strategy to address inequalities and thus it was introduced as a measure to address poverty following failures of the First Five Year plan which was not delivering as planned. The rural and urban development differences were increasing, but poverty was not reducing, and the number of local experts remained insignificant as compared to foreigners; while land and labour resources were being underutilised.

The Ujamaa Period (1967–1985)

Tanzania embraced Ujamaa in 1967, even though the idea had been contemplated over much earlier, even before its adoption as witnessed in Nyerere's own words *"no under-developed country can afford to be anything but socialist"* (Nyerere, 1961 in Ibhawoh and Dibua, 2003). Ujamaa is an African form of socialism which is different from scientific socialism as it aimed at creating an African socialist society without conflict and exploitation[21] (Ibbot, 2014: 73; Mhando, 2011; Shivji, 1974). Ujamaa was introduced by the Tanzanian ruling class as a development strategy (Mhando, 2011; Shivji, 1974). Ujamaa, being a state-centric approach, aimed to fight poverty, ignorance and diseases that were caused by many decades of colonialism exploitation and the market economy in Tanzania (Ngowi, 2009; Sandbrook, 1995; Shivji, 1974; Rodney, 1973).

Moreover, Ujamaa being an ideology, social and economic policy that governed Tanzania few years after her political independence, aimed at creating an egalitarian society with distributive justice through self-reliance (Fouéré, 2014; Ibbott, 2014; Cornelli, 2012; Ibhawoh & Dibua 2003; Nyerere, 1977). Ujamaa followed two paths to meet its objectives: nationalisation and villagisation.

---

[21]Ujamaa was an African form of socialism as it was opposed to Scientific Socialism or Marxism as the former legitimises class conflict as it "seeks to build a happy society on the philosophy of inevitable conflict between man and man i.e. the working class against the bourgeoisie." Ujamaa was against Capitalism because Capitalism "seeks to build a happy society through exploitation of man by man" Nyerere 1977, Boesen et al., 1977: 12

Nationalisation

In nationalisation, all major means of production, which included all the nine commercial banks that existed, nine milling and import-export companies, other industries included large companies, breweries, cement companies, shoes manufacturing industry, mining and tobacco companies and all institutions that were means of production were nationalised (Edwards, 2012; Ibhawoh & Dibua, 2003; Reydenfelt, 1986; Boesen, et al., 1977:11). Their ownership status changed from being private owned enterprises to being public property (Edwards, 2012; Ibhawoh, 2003; Reydenfelt, 1986; Boesen, et al., 1977: 14). Moreover, the government created a National Bank of Commerce which had monopoly power with banking and financial activities. In addition, the government assumed power over all agricultural products and so became the sole buyer of all crops (Edwards, 2012).

The private sector in socialism normally disappears, and so in Tanzania, through Ujamaa, the private sector disappeared completely and, thus the economy was consequently controlled by the state (Sandbrook, 1995:

22). Nationalisation of the private major enterprises envisioned economic growth and equity in the society. Kaijage & Tibaijuka (1996) and Rweyemamu (1973) in Sansa (2010: 89-90), argue that the main motives of nationalisation included mobilisation of surplus resources generated by nationalised enterprises so as to increase the country's productive capacity secure capital ownership for (re)-investment. This would lead to increased economic production, and use the produced surplus to meet society's needs to limit multiple forms of income transfer linked with foreign dominated market economy. It would also lead to changing the investment structure such as sector distribution and employment so as to meet national priorities, especially equal redistribution of social welfares.

In the early years of nationalisation, activities seemed to be moving on well, but at the end due to a number of causes, the running of the enterprises failed. Among other reasons, they failed due to lack of required skills to run the nationalised businesses efficiently, and corruption of the bureaucrats (Edwards, 2012; Ibhawoh

& Dibua, 2003; Sandbrook, 1995). Moreover, from the civil servants there emerged a class of "state bureaucratic capitalists"; these people used the state capital to enrich themselves and forgot deliberately about the national objectives (Shivji, 1974) and thus weakened the whole Ujamaa economic system. Nationalisation, as the objective of realising Ujamaa, ran concurrently with villagisation.

Villagisation

In the Ujamaa approach, people in the rural areas were grouped in collective villages. The government found it necessary to group people into collective villages as most people lived in scattered settlements in the rural areas (Osafo-kwaako, 2011). The villagisation process, as a self-reliance strategy, was the core of Tanzania's economic and social strategy as it aimed at revolutionising agriculture to increase production and create wealth in the country (Fouéré, 2014; Osafo-Kwaako, 2011; Ibhawoh & Dibua 2003, Boesen, et al., 1977: 13-15). Villagisation was designed as a rural development programme. It was through these Ujamaa villages that people would receive social services and work together as one society.

Osafo-Kwaako (2011), articulates that the ideal Ujamaa villages were expected to assemble farmers who would work on communal farms. Through self-reliance, they would gradually uplift their living standards, and generate surplus income to finance several basic facilities. Moreover, the Ujamaa Villages were perceived as the extension of traditional African norms of cooperation in the villages. Therefore, at first, people were not forced to join the Ujamaa villages. It was thought that they would spontaneously go to the said villages voluntarily. To persuade the rural people join the villages freely, the government provided the villages with basic services such as clean water, schools and health care facilities (Osafo-Kwaako, 2011; Sansa 2010: 91-92).

Nevertheless, many rural people were hesitant to join the Ujamaa villages because of one reason or another. Some feared that their ancestral lands would be nationalised by the government, so they resisted joining the villages freely (Ibhawoh & Dibua 2003). Therefore, in 1973, the government announced mandatory resettlement of all farmers into villages and used force to enforce the announcement (Ibhawoh & Dibua 2003). In a span of 20 months, argues Osafo-Kwaako (2011), there was a considerable transformation of the rural settings as almost 85 percent of all rural people were now living in some sort of an organised village contrary to the previous status. However, the majority of the villages did not perform as they had planned to. In some villages where there was success, there emerged a class of rich peasants "kulak," who cooperated with the bureaucrats in using the Ujamaa villages for personal interest (Shivji, 1974). In some instances, since the peasants had been forced to the Ujamaa villages, they were not well motivated. They either produced enough food only for their survival and/or when they produced surplus, they sold it to the black market instead of cooperative union official markets (Reydenfelt, 1986; Boesen, et al., 1977). Consequently, Tanzania moved from being a food exporter to a food importer (Reydenfelt, 1986).

Despite the government's efforts to realise the agriculture revolution through the Ujamaa villages, the villagisation strategy, as with the nationalization approach, failed as well. The failure was caused by a number of factors such as lack of enough resources to run the villages or mismanagement of the needed resources. Other reasons included corrupt civil servants, decline of the crops prices in the international market, drought, poor infrastructure, and rural people's unwillingness to settle in collective villages (Edwards, 2012; Ibhawoh and Dibua, 2003; Leys, 1996; Shivji, 1974).

Achievements of Ujamaa

Ujamaa, as a strategy for poverty reduction and, consequently, eradication recorded achievements and failure in different spheres of life. It addressed both income-poverty and non-income poverty in the country through the nationalisation and villagisation approaches.

On the non-income poverty indicators such as education, health care facilities, and water supply, Ujamaa improved and expanded the services to a bigger population than before. The intention as already stated was to have a fair redistribution of wealth amongst the population. Sansa (2010: 91), argues that in the education sector, education which was designed for self-reliance so as to meet the objectives of becoming a self-reliant nation, was spread to the population through several strategies.

An adult literacy campaign was designed and spread in the 1970s, including an increase of primary education enrolment which led to universal primary education in 1977, and the expansion of secondary and tertiary education. In the health sector, a universal primary health care plan, which served people with basic health services, was adopted, thus leading to the spread of rural dispensaries and health care centres in many rural areas of the country. On water supply, Kaijage & Tibaijuka (1996) in Sansa (2010: 91), maintain that the Ujamaa strategy planned to realise universal coverage by 1990 unfortunately Ujamaa did not grow that old to realise its dream.

Table 2: Tanzania: Income Poverty and Non-income poverty Indicators 1967-1971

Some Income Poverty Indicators	1967	1968	1969	1970	1971
Real GDP Growth (%)	4.8	5.1	2.3	6.0	3.8
Per capital GDP growth (%)	1.7	2.0	-0.8	2.8	0.6
Inflation, consumer, prices annual (%)	12.2	15.6	16.4	3.5	4.8
Official Exchange rate (Tsh/US $-period average)	7.14	7.14	7.14	7.14	7.14
Exports (% of GDP)	26.5	24.2	24.7	24.0	24.1
Imports (% of GDP)	26.2	26.7	24.4	28.4	33.0
Populations (millions)	12.4	12.8	13.2	13.6	14.0
Life Expectancy at birth	45.6	45.9	46.3	46.7	47.0
Primary School Enrolment (% gross)				33.8	35.2
Secondary School Enrolment(% gross)				2.7	2.7

Source: Adapted from Edwards, 2012, Table 4 and Table 5

Table 2b Tanzania: Income Poverty and Non- income poverty Indicators 1972-1975

Some Income Poverty Indicators	1972	1973	1974	1975
Real GDP Growth (%)	5.3	3.5	2.5	5.9
Per capital GDP growth (%)	2.0	0.2	-0.8	2.7
Inflation, consumer, prices annual (%)	7.6	10.4	19.6	26.1
Official Exchange rate (Tsh/US $-period average)	7.14	7.02	7.13	7.37
Exports (% of GDP)	24.6	22.4	21.3	18.2
Imports (% of GDP)	29.8	29.3	34.8	31.0
Populations (millions)	14.5	15.0	15.5	16.0
Life Expectancy at birth	47.4	47.9	48.3	48.7
Primary School Enrolment (% gross)	37.2	40.2	43.5	53.1
Secondary School Enrolment(% gross)	2.7	2.8	3.0	3.1

Source: Adapted from Edwards, 2012, Table 4 and Table 5

Table 2 and Table 3 indicate selected income poverty (economic) indicators and non-income poverty (social) indicators during the Ujamaa period. As it can be seen from the tables, the economy was growing at a very low pace, recording its lowest growth of 0.4 percent in 1977 and its highest of 6 percent in 1970. The economy never reached a growth of 7 percent during all the 19 years of Ujamaa strategy implementation. As a newly independent country, the Tanzanian economy was supposed to grow at a high rate so that it could be able to address the many ambitious plans that the Ujamaa strategy had intended to accomplish. Nonetheless, it appears that Ujamaa, as an economic strategy and policy, failed to boost necessary economic growth.

At the end of the Ujamaa strategy in 1985, most income poverty (economic) indicators scored poorly as observed in the two Tables 2 & 3. The inflation rate tripled from 12.2 percent in 1967 to 33.3 percent in 1985 while the export rate decreased from 26.5 percent in 1967 to 6.8 percent in 1985; the import rate decreased from 26.2 percent in 1967 to 16.8 percent in 1985. The reduction in import should have been good news only if exports increased; but when the import rate is compared with the export rates, one realises that the ability of the economy even to import important goods had gravely reduced by the end of the strategy. This means that at the end of Ujamaa, as an economic strategy, Tanzania failed to become a self-reliant nation as witnessed from Tables 2 and 3. Tanzania became an importer nation as its exports capabilities declined enormously while the import rates, though smaller than in 1967, were higher than export rates in 1985.

Table 3: Tanzania: Income Poverty and Non-Income Poverty Indicators 1976- 1980

Some Income Poverty Indicators	1976	1977	1978	1979	1980
Real GDP Growth (%)	5.4	0.4	1.2	3.4	3.0
Per capital GDP growth (%)	2.2	-2.8	-1.9	0.2	-0.2
Inflation, consumer, prices annual (%)	6.9	11.6	6.6	12.9	30.2
Official Exchange rate (Tsh/US$-period average)	8.38	8.29	7.71	8.22	8.20
Exports (% of GDP)	21.7	19.5	14.6	14.1	13.2
Imports (% of GDP)	23.9	22.8	29.7	26.9	26.3
Populations (millions)	16.5	17.0	17.5	18.1	18.7
Life Expectancy at birth	49.0	49.4	49.7	49.9	50.2
Primary School Enrolment (% gross)	63.1	71.1	90.7	94.2	95.6
Secondary School Enrolment(% gross)	3.2	3.3	3.3	3.4	3.3

Source: Adapted from Edwards, 2012, Table 5 and Table 6

Table 3b: Tanzania: Income Poverty and Non-Income Poverty
Indicators 1981- 1985

Some Income Poverty Indicators	1981	1982	1983	1984	1985
Real GDP Growth (%)	0.5	0.6	2.4	3.4	4.6
Per capital GDP growth (%)	-2.7	-2.6	-0.8	0.2	1.4
Inflation, consumer, prices annual (%)	25.7	28.9	27.1	36.1	33.3
Official Exchange rate (Tsh/US$-period average)	8.28	9.28	11.1	15.3	17.5
Exports (% of GDP)	12.2	8.5	8.0	9.0	6.8
Imports (% of GDP)	20.7	17.7	14.1	16.7	16.8
Populations (millions)	19.3	19.9	20.5	21.1	21.8
Life Expectancy at birth	50.4	50.6	50.8	50.9	51.1
Primary School Enrolment (% gross)	97.2	93.3	91.5	86.9	76.4
Secondary School Enrolment(% gross)	3.1	3.0	3.1	3.1	3.3

Source: Adapted from Edwards, 2012, Table 5 and Table 6

Tables 2 and 3 above show non-income poverty (social) indicators, including life expectancy at birth, primary and secondary school enrolments and the population. Life expectancy at birth kept on increasing throughout the Ujamaa policy implementation. It increased from 45.6 years in 1967 to 51.1 years in 1985. The improvement in life expectancy was influenced by the improvement of health care services, as argued by Sansa (2010: 91) that the universal health care services led to the spread of dispensaries and health care centres countrywide. The primary and secondary school enrolment increased as well. The secondary school enrolment averaged at 3.07 percent in all the 16 years since the capturing of the information. The enrolment rate rose from 2.7 percent in 1970 to 3.3 in 1985. The primary school enrolment was phenomenal as it rose from 33.8 percent in 1970 to a maximum record of 97.2 percent in 1981 and reduced to 76.4 percent in 1985. The impressive increase in the primary school enrolment can be explained by the universal primary education which was adopted in 1977.

The improvement in social indicators is astonishing as it goes contrary to economic deterioration as witnessed in Tables 2 and 3. The economy was in a weak state, yet the social indicators were performing fairly well. This mismatch between economic deterioration and social well-being improvement can be explained by the argument of Edwards (2012) that despite poor performance of Ujamaa as an economic policy, the international community continued to give aid to Tanzania. In some occasions, the international community participated in the planning and execution of some of the strategies.

In the same line of thought, we would like to applause the Ujamaa government for investing on her human development so that the people, in the future, would take full charge of their economy. Despite weak economic performance of the Ujamaa policy, the leadership thought of the future through investment in education.

Moreover, Ujamaa, as a social and political policy, is credited for being able to unite the people of Tanzania. Notwithstanding a huge number of ethnic groups, over 120 tribes, the sense of national identity amongst Tanzanians is strong. This fact has made Tanzania remain as one of those most stable countries in the continent (Erickson, 2012; Nord et al., 2009, Ibhawoh and Dibua 2003, Landau 1998).

Failure of Ujamaa

The failures of Ujamaa as an economic policy were enormous. They included significant reduction in agricultural production which was caused by a number of reasons such as poor infrastructure due to lack of maintenance which, in turn, limited distribution of products. Some farmers who were forced to move to the Ujamaa villages refused to obey the order and thus reduced or stopped farming. Matters were made worse by the decline of crop prices in the international market (Edwards, 2012). Inflation[22] went high and reached the maximum of 36.1 percent in 1984 as can be seen on table 3 above. Shortage of basic goods was severe. There was also constant blackout in all regions in the country, which limited production in the factories. Moreover, there emerged a severe black market for foreign exchange (Edward, 2012; Nord et al., 2009). Furthermore, many of the industrial projects that were financed by the international community, mostly by the Nordic countries, were facing difficulties, and the state run industries were performing below their capacity.

---

[22] Is the sustained increase in the general level of prices for goods and services. It is measured as an annual percentage increase. As inflation increases every Shilling, for Tanzanians, that one owns or buys a smaller percentage of goods or service. The value of a currency does not stay stable when there is inflation. The value of a currency is observed in terms of purchasing power, which are real goods that money can buy. When inflation goes up, there is a decline in the purchasing power of money.
(http://www.investopedia.com/university/inflation/inflation1.asp)

Furthermore, the biggest failure of them all in the Ujamaa strategy was on villagisation. Villagisation failed to work according to plan. This was supposed to be the most important approach in realising the goal of Ujamaa. It was envisioned that through villagisation, which would have stimulated industrialisation, Tanzania would become a self-reliant nation. The plans were that people would move voluntarily to the Ujamaa villages, but when the figures of compliance were low, the government applied force to the peasants (Fouéré, 2014; Edwards, 2012; Ibhawoh & Dibua 2003). The peasants retaliated in a number of ways such as selling crops to the black markets instead of official cooperative government markets (Edwards, 2012; Reydenfelt, 1986). Consequently, agricultural production and exports declined significantly, and thus as discussed by critics of Ujamaa; Ujamaa as an economic policy failed the people of Tanzania. It misused the development opportunity, de-industrialized little industries in the country, and consequently, gave rise to rural poor people and corrupt and inefficient civil servants. Conditions that continue to affect and underdevelop the country (Johnson, 2000; Scott, 1999;

47

Nursey-Bary, 1980). These Ujamaa failures should be used as a lesson when Tanzania, according to my views, searches for her soul: capitalist or socialist.

The failures that occurred during the Ujamaa era provide a good avenue for the proposed development model to learn from so that such mistakes will not be repeated once the new model is implemented. The weaknesses that occurred in the Ujamaa period while Tanzania was a developmental state are addressed in the pragmatic intervention of the proposed development model in chapter seven.

Fouéré (2014) and Edwards (2012), argue that in the late 1970s and early 1980s, the weaknesses and failures of Ujamaa became apparent, and it was necessary to change the economic policy. The changing of policy was facilitated by the relinquishing of power by President Julius Nyerere in 1985 (Tanzania Human Development Report, 2014; Edwards 2012; Wangwe, 2005; Muganda 2004). From then on, Tanzania moved from socialism to capitalism, from state-controlled and driven economy to neo-liberalism in the market oriented economy.

Capitalists in Ujamaa?

"Building a socialist nation was not a cup of tea."This was mentioned by Mwalimu Julius Nyerere in one of his political speeches made during his political life that spanned for over 40 years of active politics. He said, as we build a just and self-reliant state, there will be individuals who will side with our enemies. There will emerge individuals who will stand for capitalists and betray our intention for self-reliance. However, as a country we are determined, and by using our resources, we shall succeed. The speech (not exact words though) is interesting. It gives a picture of a politician who knew his people and the country he was building as the first citizen very well. Moreover, it reveals the deep patriotism of a genuine African leader who was aware of the resources of his country but also conscious of poverty that was rampant and could almost be smelt in the air, and felt in people's daily life.

Despite awareness of possible enemies within the house, Nyerere continued to work with individuals (not necessarily enemies) who had been trained by capitalist scholars and thus, to some extent, they too would eventually become capitalist disciples. It makes one wonder as to what was his intention to work with experts who were trained in the capitalistic system. Thus, I guess, those experts operated from capitalistic principles. Did Nyerere think that at the end, the scholars trained in the west would embrace the Ujamaa ideology? Was patriotism of early scholars and bureaucrats much stronger than their education certificates? Or since Mwalimu so much believed in Ujamaa na Kujitegemea, then he assumed and believed that Ujamaa was so strong that by "its power" these capitalists trained economists and bureaucrats would convert to the Ujamaa thinking and practice?

A typical example of economists for this argument is Professor Kighoma Ali Malima[23] (1938–1995) an economist trained at Princeton– whose dissertation was

---

[23] By all means I do not indeed to write the biography of this brilliant economist but simply point him out as an example that serves in my argument.

supervised by a well-known capitalist theorist and Nobel Prize winner Sir William A. Lewis[24]. Kighoma Malima, who was one of the first African economics lecturers at the University of Dar es Salaam, went on to become a minister of planning and finance in 1980 (Edwards, 2012). He, being trained in capitalistic settings, served his country when it was intending to become a socialist state. How did Malima reconcile his economics profession, which I think to some extent must have been influenced by his dissertation's supervisor, and that of his party's socialist ideology? This calls for an investigation, even though, I think the ultimate truth on the matter remains buried deep down in his heart. Responses and explanations from others will remain as simply opinions.

Economic Restructuring (1986 – 2005)

The Tanzanian economy continued to deteriorate due to the failure of the Ujamaa economic policies (Edwards, 2012; Nord et al., 2009). However, following changes in

---

[24] Lewis (1915-1991) An economist from St. Lucian in his theory of economic development with Unlimited supplies of Labour; he argues that least developed countries have a surplus of unproductive labour in the agricultural sector – through this surplus labour least developed countries could move from traditional to modern industrialised states
–https://www.britannica.com/biography/Arthur-Lewis
–http://onlinelibrary.wiley.com/doi/10.1111/j.1467-9957.1954.tb00021.x/abstract

political leadership in 1985, Tanzania adhered to the IMF conditions for economic recovery. Even before giving in to the IMF conditions, Tanzania had started some form of home grown structural adjustments when it adopted a National Economic Survival Program (1981-82) and continued up to 1986 (Fouéré, 2014). Nord et al., (2009), argue that as economic conditions worsened, and following continued pressure from external donors, in 1986, Tanzania gave in to the IMF conditions and introduced a comprehensive SAP called the Economic Recovery Program (ERP) which was intended to restore economic stability and quicken the structural reforms that had been started by the government.

Abugre (2000) in Oberdaberning (2010), discloses that SAPs are programs which make it possible for countries to get a loan from either the IMF or the WB. These loans are accompanied by conditions such as significant policy reforms which have to be adhered to before getting the loan. The SAP normally includes a lot of different policies which interact with each other so as to fight poverty in a given country. Policies and variables which could influence poverty and which the SAP addresses include currency devaluation, reductions in the budget deficit[25] and changes in growth rates, inflation rates and interest rates.

Edwards (2012) discloses that the bigger part of the ERP package was on currency devaluation. The Shilling devaluation would be followed by structural reforms geared to liberalize the economy, increasing efficiency and productivity and stimulating growth. In 1986, the currency was depreciated from 17 TSh per US Dollar to TSh 40 per Us Dollar, and a number of structural reforms followed in two different stages.

Nord et al. (2009) argue that the economic restructuring in Tanzania took place in two different phases – the first one starting in 1986 to 1995 and the second one in 1996 to 2006. In the first stage, a number of changes were enacted including liberalisation of exchange and trade regimes, liberalisation of

---

[25]Budget deficit is a situation when the government's spending exceeds revenues from its sources of income such as taxation, customs duties etc. In such a situation the government is obliged to borrow money from other sources so as to meet its needs.

agricultural marketing system and domestic prices, and initiation of parastatals and civil services reforms. In the second stage, more reformation continued and that included privatisation and reform of parastatals, liberalisation of financial sector, creation of market-oriented regulatory framework, trade reform as well as regional integration, reversal of fiscal dominance of monetary policy, fiscal consolidation, and sizable finance assistance from donors.

When the first phase of change took place between 1986 and 1995, some progress was recorded. However, Nord et al. (2009) argue that the large part of the economy continued to be under government control. Many parastatals and large state owned banks continued to operate under losses. The government continued to experience large budget deficits, and the economic growth continued to be slow. Nord et al (2009) argue that with the implementation of the second phase of structural reformation and privatisation, big and conspicuous progresses were noticed. These included economic growth which reached 7 percent and inflation rate dropped to a single digit rate. There emerged a strong growth of non-traditional exports and turnaround in balance of payments[26], and government international reserves increased. Part of the government's funds could now be directed towards poverty reduction programs such as MKUKUTA I and II. Creation of efficient, competitive banking systems and most sectors of the economy became more competitive and productive. Ngowi (2009) argues that following all these reforms, Tanzania has fully embraced a capitalist economy which is market-oriented and driven by the private sector. In addition, the major features of the Tanzanian economy are those of the relatively free market forces of demand and supply.

The Capitalistic Era 2000s

At the beginning of the new millennium, the Tanzanian economic policy, just like in most developing countries, changed the focus more to poverty reduction (Tanzania Human Development Report, 2014: 54). Tanzania

---

[26] A statement that summarizes an economy's transactions with the rest of the world in a specific period of time. It encompasses all transactions between a country's residents and its nonresidents involving goods, services and income; financial claims on and liabilities to the rest of the world; and transfers such as gifts. −http://www.investopedia.com/terms/b/bop.asp

followed the move that was initiated by the WB and the IMF as a strategy to reduce the debts that developing countries owe to the international financial agencies and other countries. However, this objective is addressed in the name of poverty reduction (Jules, n.d). Therefore, in the early 2000s, Tanzania signed and committed herself to implementing the UN's MDGs. Since then, Tanzania formulated development strategies aimed at poverty reduction and human development. Some of the prominent development agenda formulated in this period include the Tanzania Development Vision (TDV) 2025, the National Strategy for Growth and Poverty Reduction (NSGRP), and Kilimo Kwanza (Tanzania Human Development Report, 2014: 55-56, United Republic of Tanzania, 2012: 10-11).

TDV 2025 envisions Tanzania in the category of medium human development by 2025. It is perceived that the country will have transformed from a low productivity agricultural economy to a semi-industrialized state led by modernised and highly productive agricultural activities linking industrial and service activities in the rural and urban areas. The development indicators in the vision are:

(1) High quality livelihood,

(2) Unity, peace and stability,

(3) Good governance,

(4) Well educated and learning society,

(5) Competitive economy capable of producing sustainable growth and shared benefits (Tanzania Human Development Report, 2014; United Republic of Tanzania, 1999). MKUKUTA I & II were designed to attain goals of both the TDV 2025 and the MDGs.

According to Jules (n.d) and Tanzania Human Development Report (2014), MKUKUTA I was a program that employed neo-liberal approach which adhered to a free market economic system to address poverty reduction in Tanzania contrary to Ujamaa which employed socialistic approach in a state driven economy to address the same problem.

The basic principle of MKUKUTA I, was to achieve higher income; thus reducing poverty through balanced growth by allowing higher household incomes to

57

improve human capabilities through better education, health, nutrition and shelter. However, studies have revealed that one of the MKUKUTA I important targets of poverty reduction was not met.

CHAPTER THREE

THEORY AND PRACTICE IN ACTION

Tanzania has never isolated itself even though it has been a full independent and sovereign state since early 1960's. It has always followed the major thoughts and trends of time and put them in practice, all for the purpose of meeting her population's dream of proper human and economic development.

During the struggles for the liberation of African states, especially in the southern part of the continent, Tanzania and Dar es Salaam used to be the centre of the movement. There was what we may call *The Dar es Salaam School of Thoughts*. The politics of Nyerere, as he was among the founding thinkers of pragmatic pan Africanism, wished to see the continent full liberated. To put into practice this politics, Nyerere, amongst many other good deeds, offered land to many African fighters from a number of countries such as Mozambique, Namibia, South Africa, and on and on, to carry out their liberation activities[27]. Tanzania was such an active member in African politics. Salim Ahmed Salim[28]; a Tanzanian diplomat and son of the land, was the secretary general of the Organisation of African Unity (OAU) for twelve years. It was during his time in office that much of the liberation struggles in the continent attained its fruition. Tanzania was an active member in the Non Aligned Movement (NAM). Julius Nyerere was the first chairperson of the South Commission (1987–1990), who even after retiring from presidency in Tanzania (1985), continued to be the champion of morality[29] as a politician. For The Dar es Salaam School of Thoughts the man behind it was Hashim Mbita.

Hashim Mbita (1933–2015), born in Tabora and studied at the Tabora boys school, worked as a Civil Servant, army officer, journalist, and politician. At different

---

[27] Land to liberation movements http://www.sahistory.org.za/dated-event/former-tanzanian-president-julius-nyerere-dies

[28] Salim Ahmed Salim http://www.un.org/News/dh/hlpanel/salim-salim-bio.htm

[29] Julius Kambarage Nyerere (1922–1999) had his faults just like any other human person. However, as an African politician in the 20th century he stood above at the forefront of honest politicians who never amassed wealth for themselves. The tendency of African leaders stealing from their own people has become common in some African states. Nyerere did not steal from Tanzanians instead he led a simple life style equivalent to majority Tanzanians

periods he worked as a regional information Officer, Government Chief Press Officer, Ambassador Press Secretary to the President, and Publicity Secretary and National Executive Secretary of TANU. He also served Executive Secretary of the OAU Coordinating Committee for the Liberation of Africa from 1974 to 1992[30].

The OAU liberation Committee was hosted in Dar es Salaam by the Tanzania government at the invitation of Mwalimu Julius Nyerere who was Mbita's mentor, and teacher. The liberation Committee provided coordinated material support for the African liberation movements who had to fight for independence during a 30 year period from 1963 to 1994[31]. Hashim Mbita worked exceptionally well with all his heart, intelligence, and love for the continent. He was a true pan African nationalist. Mbita's dedication to the south liberation portrays the true image of what Tanzania gave for both

---

[30] A Pan –Africanist freedom fighter by Brig Gen (Rtd) Hashim. I Mbita, Former Executive Secretary, OAU liberation Committee featured in First Magazine
[31] Phyllis Johnson at http://www.mohammedsaid.com/2016/02/sadc-hashim-mbita-project-southern.html accessed on 24/08/2017

people's freedom and economic development in Tanzania, and in the whole continent at large.

The Development Theories

In political economy all countries need some form of a development theory to guide their path towards people's development. This chapter reveals to you the path and genuine efforts that Tanzania underwent to experiment economic development so as to let her population attain their potential in life and lead a happy life.

The Modernization Era

In the 1960s, Tanzania, like other newly independent African states, had a vision of transforming its society from an under-developed to an industrialized state by improving the socio-economic status of her citizens through service delivery, human and economic development. Immediately after independence, the country identified three arch enemies that it had to wage war against them namely; ignorance, diseases and poverty (United Republic of Tanzania, 2012:1-2; Wangwe & Charle, 2005). The philosophy guiding the development agenda at the time of her independence was none other than modernization.

When the developed world became interested in the development of the under-developed countries, industrialised states became the role models. Capital accumulation and industrialisation were the forces of the developed economies of which SSA could follow (Todaro & Smith, 2012). The modernization theory is deeply rooted in the concept of growth and economic dualism. The dualism found in the industry and agricultural sectors had been broadened to be presented as "tradition" *vis a vis* modernity. Modernization is the process of transition from the traditional society to civilization. It comprises a social and cultural framework that facilitates the development of technology. It is argued that it is through application of science and technology that under-developed countries will attain similar levels of development as industrialized economies (Siddle & Swindell, 1990).

McMillan and Harttgen (2014) and Lewis (1954) proposed the idea of a dual sector in which under-developed countries could achieve economic growth by shifting workers from the "traditional" agricultural sector into the "modern" industrial sector. Lewis (1954) claims that under-developed countries have a surplus of unproductive labour in the agricultural sector. These workers are attracted to the industry sector where there are higher wages. Lewis argues further that entrepreneurs in the industry sector will make profit which will be reinvested in the business in the form of more fixed capital. The industry's productive capacity increases and leads to a greater demand of labour. More employees will be engaged from the surplus in the agricultural sector. The process continues until all surplus workers from the non competitive agricultural sector have been engaged. The industry sector will have grown, and the economy will have moved from traditional to industrialised society.

However, critiques of modernization, including Andre Gunder Frank (1969), and I argue that modernization theory ignored the historical experience of colonialism in under-developed countries. We argue further that the existence of the under-developed countries is necessary to the development of developed economies, which extract resources from them. Therefore, it is impossible to simply transfer labour from the traditional society to the industrialised economies without affecting their relationship. In fact in such a relationship which is necessary; as there are no teachers without students or doctors without patients, the rich get richer and the poor become even poorer. From the argument it is just impossible for least developed countries to follow the same path that was followed by the developed countries to attain industrialization; for the former would need to use other countries' resources for development that is they would need to colonize other states. Thus, such critiques led to the birth of the dependency theory.

After independence in 1961, Tanzania continued with the colonial capitalist economic system which was governed by market economy. The market economy benefited only a small section of the population (Ngowi, 2009). During that economic system, farmers cultivated a number of cash crops including coffee, sisal, tobacco, cotton and on and on mainly for export and for some local industrial processing. The idea and practices of the economy tended to follow the modernisation thinking as that was the practice of the epoch. However, majority Tanzanians did not benefit from that economy, which was contrary to the objectives of fighting for independence. Thus, the government of the day called for change of approach. The failure of the modernisation theory to stir economic change and improve people's lives in the country influenced the change from the market economy to a state-led economy which was influenced by the dependency thinking of industrialisation through revolution and socialism (Arndt et al., 2016: 238; Siddle & Swindell, 1990).

The Dependency Age

The dependency theory is in line with the real history of the country as it highlights clearly the development problems in Tanzania as the country embraced the theory when it opted for African socialism, Ujamaa, as a guiding philosophy in her development agenda. Ujamaa was indeed a great original thinking and a revolutional experiment in the whole of sub Saharan Africa even though it did fail the country, and so did the dependency theory as Nyerere stepped down peacefully[32] and Tanzania was obliged to embark to neo-liberalism.

Dependency theories became popular in the 1970s. They were championed by academics of the under-developed countries (Todaro & Smith, 2009). Leading dependency theorists such as Celso Furtado, F.H Cardoso, Samir Amin, Andre Gunder Frank are concerned with the stagnation of under-developed countries. They look at under-developed countries as positioned at the boundaries of capitalist systems of production and exchange. They see economic stagnation in under-developed countries as caused by the development of capitalism in Europe. However, dependency theorists differ with scientific socialists in the belief that capitalism is arrested and will not develop further in the under-developed countries (Siddle & Swindell, 1990).

---

[32] Nyerere stepped down peacefully after serving as president for about 23 years (1962- 1985) and influenced his CCM political party to set a 5 years term limit for the next presidents in the country. He is often credited as the first African president to do so freely.

67

The dependency theorists argue that the ruling classes[33] in under developed countries have little interest in industrialising the economy of their countries because they have a beneficial relationship with the multinational companies which extract wealth from the under-developed countries and impoverishing them further. Dependency theorists believe that under-developed countries can only industrialize through revolution and socialism (Siddle & Swindell, 1990). Critiques of the theory find that theorists commit an error of treating under-developed countries as homogenous. The fact is each country has its own specific characteristics, and thus requires a development theory suitable to its needs. The dependency theory fails to come up with an alternative approach as it confines itself in the criticism of modernization.

---

[33] There are some African leaders and members of their families who possess enormous wealth which to a large extent come from their countries. It is indeed not forbidden for leaders to accumulate wealth but that should be done honestly and transparency observed in the process of wealth acquisition. We read this in a number of books such as in King Leopold's Ghost: A Story of Greed, Terror and Heroism in Colonial Africa by Hochschild, The Politics of Africa's economy recovery by Sandbrook, 1995, and on and on.

Tanzania wanted to improve rapidly the economic status of its citizens so as to meet the objectives of fighting for independence (Ngowi, 2009). The dependency theory offered such ideas that a country could industrialise through revolution and socialism (Siddle & Swindell 1990), thus following the objective of ameliorating citizens' economic status, it became logical for Tanzania to adhere to Ujamaa. When Tanzania embraced the dependency theory through Ujamaa as its guiding philosophy in the development policies, it succeeded in some areas and failed in others. Tanzania made great progress in the human development area through provision of good quality education and health care. However, its economy deteriorated badly due to weak economic policies in the Ujamaa policy (Arndt et al., 2016; Tanzania Human Development Report, 2014; Edwards, 2012). Therefore, following such failures, the country in mid-1980s resolved to neo-liberal policies to guide its economy.

The Neo-Liberalism Era

In the 1970s, pro market economists became vocal as under-developed countries were struggling to find their way few years after independence. The focus of this theory is on the relationship between the state and the market in the process of economic development (Moreira & Crespo, 2012). The central argument was that under-development in Africa was caused by the state heavy hand on markets, incorrect pricing policies that caused misallocation of resources (Todaro & Smith, 2009). Tanzania under Ujamaa went through the argued experience as the government controlled major means of the economy (Edwards, 2012; Leys, 1996; Sandbrook, 1995). The theory has three different approaches, namely; the free market approach, the public choice approach and the market friendly approach.

The Free Market Approach

The free market approach holds that markets alone are competent and capable of determining investment in new economic endeavours. The labour market responds accurately to the demands of the new industries, producers know best the demands of the market and know how to respond efficiently and profitably (Todaro & Smith, 2009). However, in under-developed countries, governments intervene in the market functions by manipulating prices of agricultural products by fixing them with low prices while industrial wages are kept high compared to agricultural prices. The government intervention distorts pattern of resource allocation and consequently, efficiency and welfare are reduced. Thus, the free market is preferred as it ensures efficiency and economic growth (Moreira & Crespo, 2012).

The Public Choice Approach

The public choice approach was introduced in the 1980s as the neo-liberalists concluded that African governments were the major cause of under-development in the continent (Moreira & Crespo, 2012). The public choice theory argues that government distorts economic activities because it is a composition of politicians and bureaucrats who work for their personal benefits. They use the power and government authority to fulfil their interests. Krueger (1990) in (Moreira & Crespo, 2012) argues that the state's economic control in under-developed countries is associated with bureaucratisation, corruption and nationalisation of private property. The neoclassical theorists prescribed liberalisation of under-developed economies as a remedy to stagnant economies. It was argued that liberalisation of the economy would encourage economic efficiency and growth. Under-developed countries were asked to privatize the state owned parastatals, promote free market, increase export diversification and welcome investors from developed countries (Edwards, 2012; Todaro & Smith, 2009).

The Market Friendly Approach

The market-friendly approach intervened as an alternative to the two previous approaches to development. This theory recognizes that markets are imperfect and, at times, the market produces imperfect goods. Theorists realised that such imperfection could be addressed by the state. The state can invest in physical and social infrastructure such as roads, railways, health care facilities, educational institutions and provision of favourable environment for private business to flourish (Skinner, 2011; Todaro & Smith, 2009).

Since mid-1980s, Tanzania adopted the neo-liberal policies to guide its development agenda following failure of the dependency theories through Ujamaa (Tanzania Human Development Report, 2014; Edwards, 2012; Wangwe & Charle, 2005). In the era of neo-liberal policies, there have been impressive economic growth in the country. However, this economic growth fails to reduce poverty significantly amongst the rural people who are the majority in the country (Arndt et al., 2016; Tanzania Human Development Report, 2014; World Bank, 2015; Kessy et al., 2013; Mashindano, 2011; Mkenda et al., 2010, Twaweza, 2009). It is more than two decades of economic liberalisation and neo-liberal policies in Tanzania, yet the majority rural people continue to be poor. This suggests inefficiency of neo-liberalism as a remedy to poverty in that sub-Saharan country, hence the call for an alternative approach to drive the development agenda in Tanzania.

How does neoliberalism operate in Tanzania, how effective is it as a tool to poverty reduction and even eradication in the country? This matter and much more are discussed in the following chapter. And as for an

73

alternative development model to address poverty squarely in the country. I invite you in chapter seven for the proposed development model

.

CHAPTER FOUR

THE FAILED MESSIAH?

When it became apparent that the Ujamaa policy was no longer effective in addressing economic problems in the country[34], a messiah was proposed and introduced to the East African state. Capitalism in the name of neo-liberalism was brought as the messiah to rescue the economic situation in Tanzania in the 1980s.

The Efficacy of Neo-Liberalism in Poverty Reduction

In the following pages we embark in discussing the efficacy of neo-liberalism in Tanzania. The chapter discusses findings on the efficacy of neo-liberalism on the country's development agenda and poverty reduction in Mandalu (2016). This discussion is the continuation of the first attempt that was made in Chapter three where the theories that Tanzania has

---

[34] As discussed in chapter 2; Ujamaa provided both ideology and economic policies to the country for about two decades from 1967 to 1985. It helped the country in a number of development indicators more specifically in non-income development indicators of education, health and water. Moreover, it has left a lasting legacy of unity amongst Tanzanians. However the model was hit hard by the Kagera war in 1978, the two severe world oil shocks in 1979, breaking of the East African community and the severe drought in the country in 1970s, and thus the Ujamaa economic policy could no longer hold.

employed in its economic trajectory were thoroughly discussed. In this chapter, I expound more on neoliberalism. I investigate what neoliberalism is, how it functions worldwide and in Tanzania, in particular, how it is integrated into the development agenda, and how does it influence and/or contribute to poverty reduction, if at all. Why is it that there is economic growth without substantial poverty reduction while neoliberalism has been the guiding philosophy, implicitly though, for nearly three decades?

To find out the efficacy of neo-liberalism on economic growth, development agenda and poverty reduction, the study expatiates first on what neoliberalism is and how it operates. There are various definitions and explanations on neoliberalism, in this book. I apply the discussion on neoliberalism as put forth by Harvey (2005). The Harvey neoliberalism definition is preferred because it is in line with the neoliberal theory as discussed in Chapter three in section 3.4 of this work and thus it follows logically the thinking of the book.

"Neo-liberalism is a theory of political economic practices that proposes that human development through well-being can best be advanced by liberating individual entrepreneurial freedoms and skills within an institutional framework characterized by strong private property rights, free markets, and free trade. The role of the state is to create and preserve an institutional framework appropriate to those practices. For instance, the state has to guarantee the quality and integrity of money. It must also set up the police, the legal system and functions required to secure private property rights and to guarantee, by force if need be, the proper functioning of the markets. Moreover, if markets do not exist then they must be created, by state action if necessary. But beyond these tasks the state should not venture. State interventions in markets must be kept to a bare minimum because, according to the theory, the state cannot possibly possess enough information to second guess market signals and because powerful interest groups will inevitably distort and bias state interventions for their own benefits" (Harvey, 2005).

The Harvey neoliberalism description reveals a clear picture of what neo-liberalism is and what it intends to do. It puts accent on individual freedom, individual property right and individual agenda as opposed to collective property rights, collective development agenda and anything collective. In Tanzania and worldwide, neo-liberalism has become an economic theory and an ideological attack on anything that deals with collective property (socialism), national development and social solidarity (Shivji, 2008). The concept of individual freedom – individualism – is overemphasized beyond the individualism of the enlightened bourgeois liberalism. Margaret Thatcher, one of the strong proponents of neo-liberalism, went even further and claimed that there was "no such thing as society. There are only individual men and women" even though she added their families later on (Furedi, 1995 in Shivji, 2008). This emphasis put on the individual poses questions on how then can a country's development agenda, which is collective in nature, be realized in a country that adheres implicitly, though, to neoliberalism? I discuss this matter extensively later on in this same chapter.

Neo-liberalism in Practice

Neo-liberalism functions through set principles which are adhered to by recipient countries for economic reformations to bear desired results as prescribed by the theory. The main principles of neo-liberalism include, but not limited to, the rule of the market, cutting down public expenditure on social services, privatisation, and elimination of public good and putting emphasis on individual freedom and responsibility. The first experimentation with neoliberalism was employed in Chile in South America. The Chilean economic program was prepared and led by economists who had been trained through US funds at the University of Chicago as part of the Cold War program so as to counteract left wing tendencies in Latin America (Harvey, 2005). What was done in Chile echoes in much of Africa today, including Tanzania (Shivji, 2008).

Working alongside the IMF, they restructured the economy according to their theories. They reversed the nationalisation and privatised public assets opened up natural resources to private and unregulated exploitation, privatised social security, and facilitated foreign direct investment and freer trade. The right of foreign companies to repatriate profits from their Chilean operations was guaranteed. Export-led growth was favoured over import substitution (Harvey, 2005).

What happened in Chile is indeed what happened in Tanzania as discussed in the economic history of the country. In 1986, when economic conditions continued to deteriorate in the country following continual pressure from external donors, Tanzania gave in to the IMF conditions and so introduced a comprehensive SAP which intended to restore economic stability and make it possible for the country to secure a loan from either the IMF or the WB. The loans were accompanied by conditions such as significant policy reforms which had to be adhered to before securing the loan. Some of the conditions included privatisation of public enterprises, ownership rights to private owners, including foreigners, elimination of trade barriers and repatriation of foreign profits. Studies have disclosed that such restructuring has been able to stimulate economic growth. However, the problem is who benefits from such economic growth recorded. This is typical of the

Tanzanian experience that followed economic and structure reformation. The economy grows as it is envisaged in economic policies such as in the MKUKUTA I strategy through neo-liberal principles. However, it does not address poverty reduction efficiently.

Neo-liberalism Practice in Tanzania

The private sector under economic reformation (neo-liberalism) was supposed to be an important partner in the implementation of the development vision 2025 and MKUKUTA I. Despite global acknowledgement of the significant role of the private sector in economic development and in the development agenda, in many sub Saharan Africa (SSA) and Tanzania in particular. The private sector, especially the one with domestic entrepreneurialism, is small and has remained at the embryonic stage (Research and Analysis Working Group, 2009: 175). The flourish and success of the private sector in an economy requires certain conditions such as peace, free market capable of regulating itself, the rule of law and an environment capable of reducing uncertainties and costs of doing business.

Tanzania, virtually since independence over five decades ago, has been a peaceful country with political stability, runs by the rule of law, has a favourable environment for investment and a flourishing private sector (Research and Analysis Working Group, 2011: 135); through the MKUKUTA I strategy, the government embraced and pledged to put emphasis on the growth of the private sector as a tool to run the market economy and economic development (United Republic of Tanzania, 2005: 57). Nonetheless, despite all that effort, neoliberalism and/or the government of Tanzania have failed to create favourable business conditions to help the entrepreneur community to grow big. Instead, only a small and less vibrant private sector can be witnessed in the country (Research and Analysis Working Group, 2009: 175). The weak domestic private sector in the age of neoliberalism reflects the same situation that Tanzania, then Tanganyika, experienced during the brief market economy era between 1961 and 1965 (Ngowi, 2009; Sandbrook, 1995). This finding on a weak private sector in the country was echoed by an interviewee, who did not want to disclose his identity, in Dar es Salaam:

> "During MKUKUTA I the private sector did not grow much as it should have grown given the strategy. There are many reasons for that; first the government did not support the sector properly because the government did not have a development model to follow. The government failed to do so because it didn't know or didn't have the rules and regulations that would have directed it on how to operate. It had just stopped being the chief overall seer of the country's economy during the Ujamaa era where businesses were run differently as compared to the open market economy. Moreover, the local business people themselves did not have the required skills, the right attitude and lacked large capital to venture in competitive business with full confidence; consequently the private sector remained dormant."

Today, the situation has been aggravated by recent poor performances, as recorded in the business indices. Since 2006, inflation has been rising, reaching 12.1 percent in 2009. Meanwhile, domestic income, as a proportion of GDP ratio, continued to be small at 15.3 percent in 2009/10, thus leading to dependency on donor countries (Research and Analysis Working Group, 2011: 135). Failure in stimulating growth of a vibrant private sector reveals inefficiencies in the operations of neoliberalism in the country. This is depicted in the recent findings of the Global Competitiveness Report (2010/11) and the Doing Business Report (2011). The Global Competitiveness Report examines the climate, conditions and business environment of world economies based on 12 indicators which are examined separately but function interdependently. From the 2010/11 report, overall, Tanzania scored 3.6 out of 7 on the Global Competitive Index (GCI) and ranked 113th out of 139 economies examined by the survey (Research and Analysis Working Group, 2011: 136–137). The table below indicates all 12 indicators used in the survey with their performances.

Table 4: Tanzania's Ranking in the Global Competitive Index

Global Competitive Index (GCI) Indicators	Rank (out of 139)	Score Scale (1-7)
GCI 2010 – 2011 (out of 139)	113	3.6
Basic requirements	116	3.6
1st Institutions	83	3.7
2nd Infrastructure	128	2.4
3rd Macroeconomic environment	115	3.9
4th Health and primary education	113	4.7
Efficiency enhancers	114	3.4
5th Higher education and training	133	2.5
6th Goods market efficiency	108	3.8
7th Labour market efficiency	77	4.3
8th Financial market development	90	4.0
9th Technological readiness	131	2.6
10th Market size	81	3.4
Innovation and sophistication factors	94	3.2
11th Business sophistication	98	3.5
12th Innovation	86	2.9

Source: Research and Analysis Working Group, 2011

From the table above, it is clear that the country has poor performance in the business environment – which is an important attribute of neo-liberalism. The Global

Competitive Report confirms findings revealed in Mandalu (2016). One of those findings is on poor quality of education in the country. Poor quality of education limits availability of future well-trained, innovative and competitive work force in both public and private sectors, and poor physical infrastructure limits economic growth. This leads to a non-vibrant private sector as it fails to attract both domestic and foreign investors who would have injected more capital which in turn would stimulate economic growth, improve efficiency in neoliberalism and thus, enhance poverty reduction.

Moreover, the Global Competitiveness Report identified the most problematic factors which limit efficiency in doing business in the private sector in Tanzania in 2010/11.

Figure 1: The Most Problematic Factors of Doing Business in Tanzania 2010/ 2011

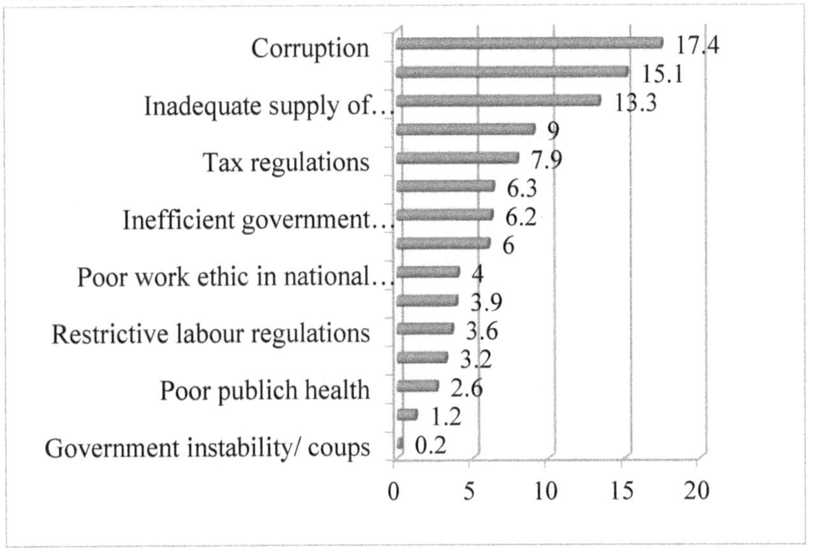

Source: Research and Analysis Working Group, 2011

Figure 1 illustrates the Global Competitiveness Report's findings for Tanzania in the 2010/11 study. Corruption was ranked as the most problematic factor in doing business followed by access to finance, poor infrastructure, tax rates and crime and theft. To attain a competitive economy and enhance substantial poverty reduction, it is necessary to address these factors effectively. This study does not dwell on the issue of corruption as this matter is treated under good governance – a wide subject that requires a proper forum for such a discussion. It is enough at this stage to mention it and call for efforts to address the problem for smooth running of the private sector in the country. The problem of poor infrastructure reappears once again in the report, and this is not by error. It is to emphasize that this is indeed a monumental problem that hinders economic growth, efficiency in neo-liberalism and leads to failure in poverty reduction. To overcome these challenges, the infrastructure question should be thoroughly addressed for weaknesses in the infrastructure sector hinder efficient economic growth as most or all economic activities become paralysed.

Doing Business in the Country

The WB and International Finance Corporation (IFC) Doing Business Report is a report that assesses national regulations that can facilitate or constrain business performance in a country. The findings from the Doing Business Report (2011) in Tanzania revealed that the major obstructions to business included difficulties in starting a business, dealing with construction permits and registering property. Further findings revealed that:

- Starting a business in Tanzania required 12 procedures. It needed 29 days and costs 30.9 percent of GNI per capita.

- Building a warehouse needed 22 procedures – it took almost a year, about 328 days and costs about 2,756.29 percent of GNI per capita; and

- Registering property needed 9 procedures, taking 73 days and costing 4.4 percent of value of the property.

The indicators that the country was ranked relatively better, as compared to others, included enforcing contracts, protecting investors and getting credit (WB & IFC 2010 in Research and Analysis Working Group, 2011: 138). Once again, the question of governance comes out clearly as it is reflected on the long bureaucracy needed to establish a business in the country. Governance is one of the clusters of MKUKUTA I. However, for the purpose of focus, this book does not discuss it, even though it is worth noting as a problem to be addressed for effective business performance, economic growth, economic development, poverty reduction and realisation of the development agenda. Regarding indicators in which the country performed well, these demonstrate and affirm that the country is run by the rule of law as it is demonstrated in the report that enforcing and protecting the private property right were highly ranked as important components in a neoliberal economy. However, in the other indicators where the country performed poorly, there is necessity for improving infrastructures to facilitate doing of business for economic growth and poverty reduction amongst people in the informal sector.

Investment Climate

In 2006, the WB carried out a survey on small, medium and large enterprises and micro-enterprises to examine the investment climate in the country. Some of the major findings were as follows. The labour productivity in the country resembles low-income economies in SSA. The value added for employees in the country was estimated to be US\$ 3000, whereas the highest value for low income economies in SSA was US\$ 4000. This means that Tanzania was not at the top level even in the low-income SSA category and that its human resource is not competitive enough. The cost of labour, which includes wages, salaries, bonuses, some other benefits and social payments, resembled other poor countries in SSA. For comparison purposes, in a medium business, labour costs are approximately at US$ 800 per employee. This is the second highest cost in the East African Community after Kenya.

Nevertheless, the most serious limitation in the private sector in the country is the shortage of skilled labour force in all levels. This is, indeed, serious. The country has one of the lowest numbers of high school students. The investment climate report justifies the finding of the study that the quality of education and number of qualified students is low. The Tanzanian government responded to the weakness by increasing enrolment in different levels of education in the country and employing more teachers (Research and Analysis Working Group, 2011: 55). However, the government's efforts to curb scarcity of skilled, innovative and competitive employees in the market have been hit by poor quality of education offered in the country. Mandalu (2016) reveals that the quality of education in the country has had poor results for several years as in primary school a number of pupils finished their studies without acquiring basic skills of literacy and numeracy, and in secondary schools, the general performance was not satisfactory. Consequently the failure of pupils and students in attaining the intended skills has direct implication on economic development for the country fails to have skilled labour force that could contribute effectively in both public and private sectors.

The Market in the Country

An effective development agenda requires a vibrant functioning market for buyers and sellers to carry out their activities thus stimulating economic growth for the agenda to be able to attain its goals. An efficiently functioning market needs strong institutional oversight, the establishment and enforcement of property rights and contracts, competition and consumer protection and information systems to reduce the gap between buyers and sellers. In SSA and in Tanzania, oversight institutions are not well equipped to perform their functions effectively and are often unrealistic in the market demands (Research and Analysis Working Group, 2009: 176-177).

The nature of the market in Tanzania has been changing since the beginning of neo-liberalism at the end of the 1980s (Tripp, 1997; Gibbon, 1995 in Tanzania Human Development Report, 2014). Economic liberalisation has led to rapid growth of the informal sector in the country. Moreover, the informal sector has become identical with self-employment which, unfortunately, is responsible in the generation of poor quality jobs which pay little wages to the workers (ILO, 2014). The changing market in the neoliberalism era has greatly influenced the employment sector. Economic liberalisation led to the expansion of formal manufacturing industries. However, the manufacturing sector has not generated substantial employment opportunities. Businesses established since 2005 contributed to only 11 percent of total industrial employment. This suggests that those businesses, while contributing to economic growth, concentrated in capital intensive activities which create minimal employment opportunities (UNIDO, 2013). The most notable sector in this case is the mineral industry, which grew exceptionally well but contributed very poorly in employment-generation, thus leading to failure in the poverty reduction agenda.

Figure 2: Average Annual GDP Growth Rate, 2000 - 2010

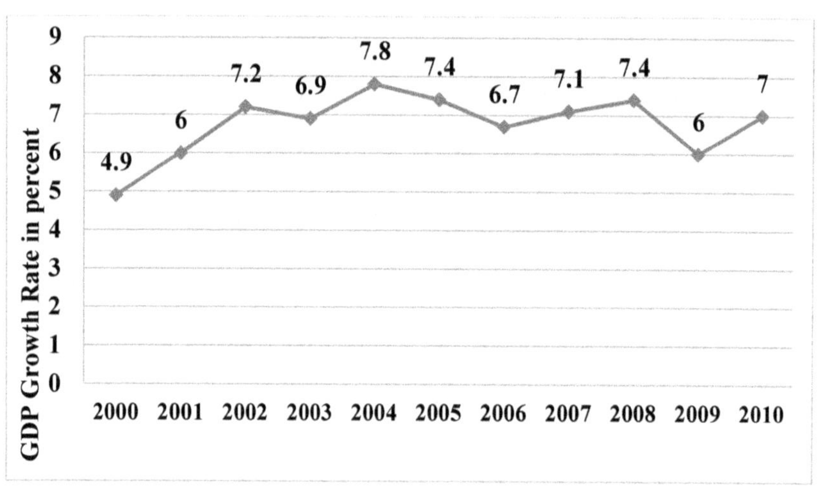

Source: Research and Analysis Working Group, 2011, Figure 1

Neoliberalism is felt in the informal sector employment which has been expanding; however, the sector faces the challenge of accuracy as capturing of exact figures is difficult. The informal employment accounted for 8.8 percent of total employment in 1990/91, 9.3 percent in 2000/01 and 10.1 percent in 2006 (Tanzania Human Development Report, 2014: 41). The informal economy in the country has expanded so much that it is estimated to be a source of income to about 94 percent of the workforce in the country (ILO, 2010). This situation is alarming as many of the informal activities in the country do not have access to necessary services for production. The growth of such a large informal economy is viewed by some analysts as a state failure. While it is known that the informal economy caters for many households, productivity in those informal firms is low due to unequal access to services. Without formal legislation, access to services is undoubtedly restricted. Nevertheless, the relationship between productivity and the formal status of a firm is complicated. Operating a firm that conforms to national business regulations by itself does not guarantee better access to required services and high profit. Remarkably, the difference in productivity between formal and informal businesses in East Africa and Tanzania, in particular, is not as serious as in Southern Africa. The reason is that informal businesses in East Africa obtain limited government assistance as compared to Southern Africa (Gelb et al., 2009 in Research and Analysis Working Group, 2011: 126)

95

Private Property Right and Free Markets

Neo-liberalism, though not declared out explicitly by relevant authorities, seemingly is the official path that the country adheres to as a development model and seems to have been integrated with the national development agenda through MKUKUTA I for the purpose of poverty reduction. The country changed from socialism to capitalism in the name of neoliberalism in 1986 (Tanzania Human Development Report, 2014: 51, United Republic of Tanzania, 2012: 9; Ngowi, 2009; Mbele, 2005; Wangwe & Charle, 2005). Notwithstanding, in this book, we find it to be a total contradiction. It is a contradiction because neoliberalism emphasizes on personal values such as individual prosperity through one's own entrepreneurial talents, hard work and protection of his/her property and individual firms, whereas MKUKUTA I aimed at creating collective benefits by reducing poverty in a population for all individuals. However, this agenda contradicts the principles of neoliberalism discussed earlier.

This contradiction, between neo-liberal principles and MKUKUTA I strategy, partly explains why despite impressive economic growth reported by a number of studies (Tanzania Human Development Report, 2014; Wuyts & Kilama 2014; Martins, 2013; Mashindano et al., 2013; Mkenda, Luvanda & Ruhinduka, 2010; Nord, R., et al., 2009), poverty does not reduce significantly in the country. In a recent study by the World Bank, this proposition is affirmed. Economic reforms and the recent economic growth in Tanzania have not led to the expansion of the domestic private sector. The growth in the private sector has been dominated by very few individual large firms, thus limiting poverty reduction as wealth is accumulated by few individuals. The dominance of few larger firms in the manufacturing sector is demonstrated by the presence of about five or six companies that dominate almost half of the manufactured products in Tanzania (World Bank, 2011 in Research and Analysis Working Group, 2011: 127). From this finding, it follows that the country's economy may continue to grow, but poverty amongst the poor may continue as well. This finding was echoed by an Interviewee in Dar es Salaam.

97

"Neo liberalism in the name of open market economy for our country is necessary for more rapid growth and poverty alleviation. Moreover, this is the trend of world economies and there is no way that we can afford to isolate ourselves as an island when it comes to the type of economy. It is also true that the open market economy has greatly contributed to economic growth but also to the huge number of poor people in the country. It is so because we did not regulate it well enough. We need to continue with an open market economy which will attract more foreign investors but the government should be in the position to check and regulate it closely for benefits of both investors and the local population just like what did the East Asian Tigers. If we fail to regulate it then only a few individuals will get richer and the rest will remain poor or even become poorer."

The most recent national data available on household income poverty were those of 2007. Poverty estimates indicated significant economic growth since 2000, as depicted by figure 2 above. However, the growth did not translate into poverty reduction whereas the percentage of the population below the basic needs poverty line reduced only marginally from 35.7 percent in 2000 to 33.6 in 2007 and on food poverty, it decreased only slightly to 16.6 percent in 2007 from 18.7 percent in 2000. Thus, with such results, the MKUKUTA I targets were not attained (United Republic of Tanzania, 2012: 12; Research and Analysis Working Group, 2011; Research and Analysis Working Group, 2009). Findings reveal that the failure in substantial poverty reduction amongst the poor in the country was perpetuated by either inefficiency in the implementation of neo-liberalism in Tanzania or by weaknesses of neo-liberal policies. At this juncture, there is need of taking a case study on neo-liberalism in Tanzania. Future studies need to examine closely and separately neoliberalism in Tanzania its success and failure as related to economic development and poverty reduction. Neo-liberal policies, in principle, favour a few individuals through their firms to manipulate the country's wealth and leave behind a bigger population in poverty. To address the imbalance and to be able to fight poverty effectively, the country needs to come up with a new development model.

CHAPTER FIVE

A DILEMMA?

SOCIALIST or CAPITALIST?

Most and indeed all countries in the world should have their development plans which give direction to the development of the said countries. Sovereign states in the world have rights and responsibilities that they deserve and got to fulfill respectively. A development agenda is one of the important responsibilities that countries have to fulfill.

The UN (2007: 11-12), defines development agenda as a comprehensive set of development goals meant to address a number of intertwined issues such as poverty reduction, gender equality, social integration, health, education, employment and much more. It can be used as a framework for development at the country, regional or even global level. For attaining desired development results in a country, a development agenda is required to be a country's own prepared instrument. The UN (2003: 5-6) in the Monterrey Consensus emphasises that a development agenda belongs to a country and, therefore, preparation of a country's development agenda is a country's own responsibility emerging from the consequence of sovereignty of a country. It re-emphasises that each *"country has a primary responsibility for its economic and social development, and the role of national policies and development strategies cannot be overemphasised."* However, it is advised that while a development agenda addresses country's own issues, it should try as much as possible to adhere to world needs as well since countries are linked to the global economic system.

The Tanzania's development agenda has, for years, been aiming at poverty reduction. Immediately after independence, the Tanzanian government called for war against what it called arch enemies, namely poverty, ignorance and diseases. It was argued that eradication of poverty would facilitate the fight against the other two enemies easily (United Republic of Tanzania, 2012:

101

1-2; Sansa, 2010; Ngowi, 2009). This agenda was not achieved because of a number of reasons. The time frame work was short, and the major reason was that the government did not have access to the economic system of the time (Ngowi, 2009; Kaiser 2007). In 1967, Tanzania formulated Ujamaa as a comprehensive set of goals which aimed to eradicate poverty and create a just society through building a self-reliant nation (Fouéré, 2014; Ibbott, 2014: 69-70; Edwards, 2012; Sansa, 2010; Ngowi, 2009). While Ujamaa registered successes in social political arena, it failed in the economic sphere following weak economic policies and external forces (Tanzania Human Development Report, 2014: 50-51; Edwards, 2012). In the 2000s, the global development agenda focused on poverty reduction in the world, especially in the developing countries by addressing the MDGs, and Tanzania came up with her own Development Vision 2025.

The development agenda 2025 envisages Tanzania in the category of medium human development by 2025. It is perceived that the country will have graduated from a low productivity agricultural economy to a semi-industrialized one led by modernized and highly productive agricultural activities linking industrial and service activities in the rural and urban areas (Tanzania Human Development Report, 2014: 54-55; United Republic of Tanzania, 2012: 2). A number of strategies and policies have been formulated as conduits of the agenda. MKUKUTA I was one of the strategies formulated to work for five years (2005 to 2010).

The constitution (1977) maintains that Tanzania is a socialist democratic state where as the official state's website states that it is an economy led by the market economy driven by the private sector (actual it is a capitalistic state in practice).

What Development Philosophy for Tanzania?

Tanzania's development model has not been explicitly stated and thus, this lacuna compels for a logical explanation on the matter. On the subject of a development model, there is conflict between theory and practice in the country. In theory, Tanzania is "a democratic, secular and socialist state which adheres to multi-party democracy" (United Republic of Tanzania,

103

The Constitution, 1977: 3.-(1)), whereas, from the official government website, Tanzania follows a market economy driven by neo-liberal policies (capitalist). Since mid-1980s, the economy has transformed from being state-controlled to market-oriented. The private sector is regarded as the powerhouse of growth, and measures are progressively being taken to enhance its role and participation. The Public Private Partnership is recognised as an important aspect in stimulating growth, development and poverty reduction.[35]What is published on the website seems to be in practice since the country observes neo-liberalism which, in many scopes including ideology and practice, is contrary to socialism announced in the constitution. What we know for sure is that the two models cannot be employed concurrently without stating this officially and initiate pragmatic strategies. However, the findings from some academic documents and practices in the economy; it is clear that the government consciously followed neo-liberal policies when it was pressured by the international community (Edwards, 2012).

---

[35]Tanzanian development model at http://www.tanzania.go.tz/home/pages/222 accessed on 1st July 2015

In addition, the government has been performing extremely well in the implementation of neo-liberal policies, which led to impressive economic growth in the country (Tanzania Human Development Report, 2014: 23; United Republic of Tanzania, 2012: 11; Wobst, 2001), even though the growth has not had significant impact on the poor. Therefore, given the evidence from academic documents and government practice, we confirm that Tanzania adheres to neo-liberal policies and thus a capitalistic development model to meet the TDV2025. However, our certitude as to what development model the country adheres to is put to the doubt by the country's constitution which clearly pronounces that the country follows a socialist development model, according to article 3.-(1) of the same constitution.

The contradicting statements of the constitution, government website and practices can be understood through a brief economic history of the country. From 1967 up to 1985, it was clear that the country followed or tried to follow a socialist development model and that can be witnessed through official documents,

105

government practices of the time and the country's constitution. However, since the second phase government, in 1986, the development model that the country follows has not been as clearly stated as was done by the government before. In fact, even as discussion in this book continues, the Tanzanian constitution of 1977 continues to acknowledge Ujamaa and self-reliance as the official development model of the country even though the practices contradict with it.

Normally, in a socialist development model, a state assumes major economic roles such as economic regulation, planning and becomes entrepreneurial, thus leading to the weakening or complete disappearance of the private sector (Sandbrook, 1995). In this model, the intention of appropriating the economy is good as the state envisages attainment of socio-economic well-being of all her citizens. As was the plan in the country. Tanzania, under Ujamaa in 1967 – 1985 behaved in that way. Unfortunately, due to a number of reasons, both internal and external, as discussed earlier, the behaviour led to catastrophic socio-economic results

(Tanzania Human development Report, 2014: 50-51; Ngowi, 2009). Such consequences forced the state to adhere to neo-liberal conditions. In a neo-liberal development model which is capitalist in nature, a state behaves in such a way that the economic system allows the private sector to own and control the use of property according to their interest, and businesses are governed by the market rules of supplies and demands. Moreover, the state plays the role of creating favourable conditions and necessary infrastructures for businesses to run smoothly (Scott, 2006). This is what Tanzania has been practising for the past three decades, as discoursed earlier.

To put things in the right perspective with regard to theory and practice of which development model the country follows, the study reveals that for decades now, the country has been implementing a number of policies intended to enable economic and political liberalisation. Despite close relationship with countries that adhere to the socialistic development model for finance and technology assistance, such as China, Tanzania's present economic development model, in practice, seems to be capitalistic and influenced by the neo-liberal paradigms that have been advocated by its development partners since mid-1980s and in the 1990s (Green, 2013a). The process of neo-liberalism in Tanzania is financed by the west and world-leading financial institutions that happen to be pushing for the spread of neo-liberalism in the world as well. In addition to the standard neo-liberal package of governance reforms, including decentralisation, Tanzania has implemented policies envisioned to move to the capitalistic market economy and emphasise on private property rights (Tripp, 1997; Ponte, 2002; Lysons & Msoka, 2010 in Green, 2013a).

The discussion in chapter four revealed that neo-liberalism is opposed to anything collective, yet the mother law in the country affirms that Tanzania follows a socialist model which is collective in nature. Thus, the theory and practise on a development model in the country need to be reconciled and be one, otherwise poverty eradication can never be realised. This finding is shocking and indeed disturbing but that is the truth of affairs in the country. No matter how one analyses the situation, it is evident that the country has not had a specific development model since mid 1980s and thus the need for action to rescue the country and her population. This explanation of lack of a development model is surely alarming, how come that the country has all the governance machinery but the question of a clear and distinct development model has not been addressed squarely for over three decades?

CHAPTER SIX

LEARNING FROM OTHERS

No man is an island, thus goes an English saying which emphasises on cooperation between individuals, and in our case it is among states. To put things in the right perspective with regard to theory and practice of which development model the country follows, I inform you that for decades now, the Tanzanian economy has been implementing a number of policies intended to enable economic and political liberalisation.

Despite close relationship with countries that adhere to the socialistic development model for finance and technology assistance, such as China, Tanzania's present economic development model, in practice, seems to be capitalistic and influenced by the neo-liberal paradigms that have been advocated by its development partners since mid 1980s and in the 1990s (Green, 2013a). The process of neo-liberalism in Tanzania is financed by the west and world-leading financial institutions that happen to be pushing for the spread of neo-liberalism in the world as well. In addition to the standard neo-liberal package of governance reforms, including decentralisation, Tanzania has implemented policies envisioned to move to the capitalistic market economy and emphasise on private property rights (Tripp, 1997; Ponte, 2002; Lysons & Msoka, 2010 in Green, 2013a). Recently, however, the government introduced a new development model designed in the East and employed in Malaysia, the Big Results Now (BRN).

In the financial year 2013/14, the government of Tanzania, in its continuous efforts to eradicate poverty and ensuring better life to all Tanzanians, adopted the BRN strategy from the Malaysian development model as an integral part of the TDV 2025 (Coulson, 2014; Balozi et al., 2014). This model emanates from a country whose economy is strongly planned, protected and directed by the government (Coulson, 2014) whereas Tanzania, as observed in the discussion above, in theory, is a government-planned economy. Notwithstanding Tanzania is a free market economy in practice.

111

The South Korean Development Model

The economic development of South Korea is often termed as a "man-made" miracle. It is a miracle in the sense that in the span of three decades the country was able to achieve a successful structural transformation that is from a traditional economy to a modern industrialised state. Many industrialised countries took almost a century to achieve what South Korea did in three decades. The transformation was, moreover, achieved with a degree of relatively equitable income distribution by international standards. Up to the 1960s, South Korea represented a true image of underdeveloped economy based on subsistence agriculture with all the difficulties facing a developing country as we know it today (Kim, 1991).

South Korea is poor in natural resources. Only about 30% of the land area is cultivatable and the arable land per farm household ranks among the lowest in the world (currently less than a hectare). Korean society was traditional, feudalistic, agrarian, and isolated from the West until the late nineteenth century. Japanese colonial rule during the period 1910 to 1945 brought both exploitation and modernisation, influencing the country's future course of development. The small infrastructural base built during Japanese rule was mostly destroyed during the Korean War of 1950-53 (Kim, 1991; Korea.net n.d). The country's per capita income in the early 1960s was lower than those of Haiti, Ethiopia, and Yemen (Kim, 1991)

In the early 1960s, the country pushed ahead with export-oriented economic development plans. At first, the country major export items were mainly light industrial products manufactured in small factories, or raw materials. In the 1970s, the country invested in heavy chemical facilities and laid the basis for the export of heavy industrial products. At present, the country has a number of industries that boast solid international competitiveness, such as the shipbuilding, steel, and chemical industries. The foundation of such strong competitiveness was built around that time.

In 1996, the country became the 29th country to join the Organisation for Economic Cooperation and Development (OECD), which is largely composed of industrialised countries. The country gradually established an export-oriented economic structure centered on large businesses in the process of pursuing growth as a country with insufficient capital and resources. Multinationals came to dominate industry, while the country economic structure became heavily reliant on exports and imports, leaving it vulnerable to external conditions.

In 1997, a foreign exchange crisis hit the country, forcing it to turn to the IMF for a bailout. It was the first trouble the country had to face after years of rapid economic growth. The country took radical step of driving poorly performing industries out of the market and pushed ahead with industrial restructuring. In only two years, the country regained its previous growth rate and price levels as well as a current account balance surplus. In the process, about 3.5 million people joined in the campaign to collect gold to help the government repay the fund borrowed from the IMF. A total of 227 tons of gold were collected. The world marveled at the Korean people voluntary participation in the determined effort to repay its national debts.

After overcoming the economic crisis, the South Korean economy continued to register solid growth. By 2010, South Korea emerged as the world 7th largest exporting country. From 2011 to 2013, the total volume of the country exports and imports stood at US$1 trillion. Thus, the country became the world 9th country to attain the target of US$1 trillion in annual foreign trade. The country foreign currency reserves stood at US$363.6 billion as of the end of December 2014, and the country is in a sufficiently stable position to cope with a foreign exchange crisis, with the percentage of its short-term foreign debts being 31.7% in 2014 (Korea.net. n.d).

The Malaysian Development Model

Malaysia covers an area of 330,323 square kilometers and lies entirely in the equatorial zone; with temperatures throughout Malaysia varying between 21°C to 32°C. The country is composed of 13 states. Malaysia is a multi-ethnic country with the principal ethnic groups of Malay, Chinese and Indian. Other significant groups are the indigenous people of Sabah and Sarawak, including Kadazan Dusun, Bajau and

115

Murut in Sabah as well as Iban, Bidayuh and Melanau in Sarawak.

Malaysia practices a system of Parliamentary democracy with constitutional monarchy. It has three branches of government – the Executive, the Legislature and the Judiciary. The Malaysian Parliament is made up of His Majesty Yang di-Pertuan Agong, the Senate (Upper House) with 70 members and the House of Representatives (Lower House) with 222 members. Out of the 70 senators in the Senate, 44 are appointed by His Majesty the king while 26 are elected by the State legislatures. The general election for the 222 members of the lower house is held every five years. The last general election was held in 2013 (Malaysian Gov 2016).

Malaysia is an upper middle income country, and in the four groups of the UNDP's human development index it is in category two of high human development. Life expectancy at birth is at 74.7 years, expected years of schooling for children is at 12.7, the mean schooling years at 10 and the national gross income per capita

(PPP \$) is at 22,762 (Human Development Report, 2015)

Malaysia has relied heavily on income from its natural resources to engineer successful diversification into manufacturing and sharply increased incomes for all ethnic groups. The country has managed to arrive at the state where it is today. Thanks to a number of strategies and hard work put in to meet the needs of all people in the multi ethnic islands of Malaysia. One of the strategies that we wish to highlight briefly though, is the Big Results Now (BRN)

The BRN is a Malaysian development model which relies on implementing new working methods in specific timeframes for efficient delivery of a required national development vision. The strategy was created in 2009 to encourage the country become a high income economy by 2020. It is due to the model and other strategies that Malaysia is classified as an industrialised economy (Balozi et al., 2014). Malaysia is an upper-middle income country which, before independence in 1957, was a low-income agrarian

117

economy whose major economic activities involved mainly the agriculture of rubber and tin as cash crops. The business class was of small size, largely localised and generally family-based. With time, the economy diversified beyond agricultural and primary commodities to the extent that manufactured goods now contribute to a much larger share of GDP and total exports (Balozi et al., 2014; Yusof & Bhattasali, 2008).

Since 1970, Malaysia based its economic development strategy on three long-term policies: the New Economic Policy 1970-1990, the National Development Policy 1990-2000 and the National Vision Policy 2001-2010. While the accent on these economic development policies was on economic growth, the Malaysian goal has always been on more equitable income redistribution that benefits citizens of all ethnic groups in the country. The emphasis on equitable income redistribution in the country was influenced by ethnic disputes caused by economic inequalities in the country in 1969. Thus since then, all government economic plans have geared to meeting economic equality of all people (Yusof & Bhattasali, 2008).

The economic success in Malaysia has been propelled by economic diversification done over time in two economic sectors. The first diversification was from rubber into the cultivation of palm oil on a large scale for business, and the second was on the diversification away from primary into secondary industries, especially manufacturing. The Malaysian success in becoming an upper-middle income economy and an industrialised economy has been possible because of the well-governed, planned and executed economic policies over the past five decades. Malaysia has been a state-led economy all along the past fifty years (Balozi et al., 2014; Yusof & Bhattasali, 2008) Therefore, as the Tanzanian government embraces the BRN as a development model to reach its TDV 2025, it needs to examine its policy implementing institutions and type of economy that the model encounters in the country.

The Rwandan Development Model

As we write the pages of this book, Rwanda is yet to attain the level of industrialisation. In fact it is still at the low Human Development Index level as according to the UNDP benchmark. According to the 2015 report;

Rwanda is ranked at 163 in a list of 188 states. It shares the same position with Uganda and Haiti which is above both East African states of Rwanda and Uganda. Haiti, at US$ 1,669, has higher gross income per capita than Rwanda and Uganda and life expectancy is at 62.8 years where as Uganda has a relatively low life expectancy (58.5 years) as compared to the other two countries. Rwanda has a life expectancy of 64.2 years, mean years of school 3.7, expected years of schooling 10.3, and the Gross National Income per capita of US$1,458. From the data above Rwanda performs better in health and education even though it is still an under developed economy.

Despite being in the category of low human development countries I take Rwanda as a role model in economic development in sub-Sahara Africa because of the zeal that country and her leadership have for development of her people. In a period of less than thirty years since the genocide tragedy that claimed lives of many innocent people, it has been able to make tremendous economic progress that other relatively peaceful and calm states in the continent have not been able to register.

Rwanda has been able to make substantial progress. The most remarkable progress was in poverty reduction. The overall real GDP growth has averaged 8 percent per year for several years. The percentage of the population living in poverty has reduced from 56.9 percent in 2006 to 44.9 percent in 2011. The reduction is translated into 1 million people out of a total population of about 10.7 million emerging from poverty in a period of five years. Moreover, the number of people living in poverty fell from 37 percent in 2006 to 24 percent in 2011 (Crisafulli & Redmond, 2012).

The recorded achievement has been possible, despite the fact that Rwanda is a land locked country.It does not have much natural resources. All has been possible due to the great asset of friends. Rwanda has an ever growing network of well-placed friends such as Tony Blair (former British Prime Minister), Rick Warren ("Purpose Driven Pastor"), Rob Glaser (Real Networks founder and CEO), Eric Schmidt (Google CEO) Chu,

(2009). Apart from the aforesaid reasons Rwanda's real mitochondria is its development model that guides all the country's development plans, dreams and operations.

The Rwandan development agenda is outlined in the framework entitled 'Rwanda Vision 2020'. The development model introduces or identifies who a Rwandese is[36], while demonstrating ambition and imagination in overcoming poverty and division. The mission intends to attain the per capita income of a middle-income state in an equitable way, and the aspiration to become a modern, strong and united nation, without discrimination amongst its citizens[37]

The Rwandan development model is made up of six pillars.These are good governance and a capable state; transformation of agriculture into a productive, high value, and market oriented sector; efficient private

---

[36] This is important and indeed necessary as it should be used as a strategy to heal the wounds of the past. The Rwanda Vision 2020 claims that the artificial differences that segregated the Rwandese were created by colonialists for their own interests. I concur with this move that aims at unifying these people who all of them speak the same language.
[37] Republic of Rwanda, 2000, Rwanda Vision 2020, Ministry of Finance and Economic Planning

sector-led development; human resource development and a knowledge-based economy through education, health and technology skills; infrastructure development which includes transportation, energy, water, and information and communications technology (ICT) networks; and promotion of regional economic integration and cooperation[38].

Critique on the Rwandan Leadership

Despite the progress recorded in Rwanda in a relatively short period of time since the 1994 genocide, leadership in the country is criticised for restricting some human rights. The effects of restrictions are manifested on weak civil society, freedom of media and on and on.

The human rights (HRW) watch argues that the civil society in Rwanda is weak, due to many years of state intimidation and interference. The government remains hostile to criticism of its human rights record and strongly favours service-delivery over independent

---

[38] Crisafullis&Redmond, 2012,The Rwanda Model: Focus on Poverty, entrepreneurship, human capital, Institutions, and Accountability accessed at http://www.americanoutlook.org/rwanda-model.html

human rights reporting or advocacy. Difficult registration requirements and bureaucratic obstacles have also prevented human rights groups from operating effectively.

Moreover, on freedom of media the HRW claims that only few Rwandan journalists challenge official government policies or investigate allegations of human rights abuses, especially against senior government officials. Many journalists engage in self-censorship. However, some radio and television debates and call-in programs have occasionally allowed space for discussion of more sensitive topics, such as the constitutional changes, the role of journalism, and illegal detention in the so-called transit centers (HRW, 2017).

Critique of the Malaysian and South Korean Models

The Malaysian government (author of the BRN) for the past fifty years has exercised a state-centric planned economy and experienced economic success whereas Tanzania, in the past fifty years, has had both state-planned and market-led economies with limited economic success. The Republic of Korea, whose development model we in this book propose for the Tanzanian government to tailor its own, followed a state-planned and controlled economy while implementing policies and practices influenced by both dependence and neo-liberal theories to become an industrialised economy. According to UNDP's standards, economies are measured and classified according to three development indicators, namely income, health and education. Income is measured through the purchasing power parity (PPP), health is checked on life expectancy, and education is measured on the expected numbers of years at school.

South Korea is now an industrialised country with a PPP exceeding $ 27,000 as per 2008 statistics and $ 30,345 by 2013. By 2004, the country was in the list of the world's countries with the highest enrolment rates in tertiary education, with graduates specialising in technical fields. By 2008, life expectancy reached 80 and 81.5 years by 2013. It is ranked high in the Human Development Index. In the new Human Development Index introduced in 2010, South Korea came immediately after Japan in the countries' ranking. Moreover, exports in the manufacturing industry, particularly in electronic goods, motor vehicles and in high technology have grown at an extraordinary rate in the country (Human Development Report, 2014: 160; Todaro & Smith, 2012: 675). Since Tanzania has experienced both state planned and market-led economies, then it is well equipped to adapt and adopt successfully the Korean development model to eradicate poverty and industrialise the country.

Both countries South Korea and Malaysia have been successful economically. However, they are not very strong democratic countries which would have substantiated logically the call for African countries in becoming democratic developmental states. South Korea is much better than Malaysia in democratic practices and thus could offer a benchmark for SSA and Tanzania to learn from. South Korea made the transition to democracy in 1987. In 2007, South Korea experienced proper democracy when the opposition candidate won 49 percent of the votes over 26 percent of the candidate of the ruling power (Chaibong, 2008).

Malaysia on the other side has not done well in democracy. The ruling party led by the United Malays National Organisation has been in power since independence in 1957. The country, although it is exemplary of national unity in the region, has not been observing important political principles and human rights such as freedom of speech and assembly (Holik, 2011). Tanzania and the SSA region are urged to become democratic developmental states. Thus from this brief overview of democracy in the two nations, the study urges Tanzania to follow the South Korean model which seems to have a brighter future both in economy and democracy.

CHAPTER SEVEN

THE DEVELOPMENTAL STATE

From the development theories studied in chapter three, we realise that there is no single theory that has been able to address under-development effectively in the country. Consequently, an alternative approach is necessary. The scrutiny of development theories exposes the development role that Tanzania and development partners have to play for the development of the country. In this book, I urge the Tanzanian government to reposition itself and become a developmental state since historical evidence depicts that African states are capable of becoming developmental states like their East Asian counterparts (Hofisi, 2013; Mkandawire, 2001). A developmental state takes an active role in planning and acting in the development process of its economy; through diversification of export structures, industrialisation and engagement in new international economic order through negotiations with industrialized economies

(Ubhenin & Edeh, 2014). Even though Tanzania has to take its development role at hand, partnership with industrialised countries is important as it helps in attracting foreign investment, application of science and technology in the industry sector and stimulation of a vibrant private sector.

Thus, while calling for Tanzania to become a developmental state, we also propose the fusion of dependency and neo-liberalism theories to create a dependency-neo-liberalism amalgamation alternative approach to drive the development agenda in Tanzania. This alternative approach is informed by the South Korean experience. South Korea adhered and integrated ideas from both the dependency school advice on industrialisation strategies, state intervention and neo-liberalism strategies such as institution reforms, use of innovation and technology in the local industry (Kasahara, 2013; Heywood, 2013; Hansen, 2010). The input from the two schools of thought saw South Korea succeed to industrialisation, an experience that can be realised in Tanzania as well.

The Developmental State

Kasahara (2013) defines a developmental state as that which facilitates structural transition from a traditional/agricultural to a modern/industrial society. The developmental state is expected to take the role of restructuring the national economic system for industrial development. In most cases, the facilitation of growth is influenced by accumulation of agricultural surplus that can be invested for the development of an industrial society. This thinking is related to the Lewis (1954) argument of modernization based on unlimited supply of surplus labour from the non-productive agricultural sector. Mkandawire (2001), on the other hand, defines a developmental state as an ideology-structure nexus. As an ideology, the developmental state is principally one whose ideology underpins 'developmentalism' because it conceives its objective as that of ensuring economic development, usually understood to mean high rates of accumulation and industrialisation. Castells (1992) in Mkandawire (2001) and Mkandawire (2001) in Hofisi (2013) maintain that such a state establishes, as its principle of legitimacy, its ability to promote sustained development, understanding by development the steady high rates of economic growth and structural change in the productive system, both domestically and in its relationship to the international economy.

The developmental state as a structure emphasises on capacity to implement economic policies 'sagaciously' and effectively. Such capacity is determined by various factors including institutional, technical, administrative and political (Mkandawire, 2001). Undergirding all these is the autonomy of the state from social forces so that it can use these capacities to devise long-term economic policies unencumbered by the claims of myopic private interests[39]; it is usually assumed that such as state should be a 'strong state' in contrast to what Gunnar Myrdal (1968) referred to as the 'soft state' that had neither the administrative capacity nor the political will to push through its developmental project. Finally, the state must have some social anchoring that prevents it from using its autonomy in a

---

[39] Private businesses are by nature competitive and many of them tend to be effective as the aim is profit making. Such organisations have private objectives which are beneficial to a limited number of individuals this is the reason why the state should intervene for the interest of all citizens

predatory manner and enables it to gain adhesion of key social actors (Kasahara, 2013; Mkandawire, 2001).

On the state and development in Africa, there are a number of opposing discussions. One outstanding feature in those discussions is the disjuncture between an analytic tradition insisting on the impossibility of developmental states in Africa and a prescription literature presupposing their existence. The analytical tradition which argues for the impossibility of the developmental states in Africa is mainly based on a number of reasons including, but not limited to: (i) dependence, (ii) lack of ideology, (iii) softness of the African states, (iv) lack of technical and analytical capacity, (v) past poor performance, and (vi) mismatch between international and local policies (Mkandawire, 2001). The prescription literature and I believe in the possibility of developmental states in the continent.

While it is true that African states are the least developed states in the world, the analytic traditional view on Africa's impossibility of developmental states is, however, and to a large extent, wrongly informed.

I discuss some of the misinformation about the continent briefly though, as our area of focus in the book is mainly on Tanzania. Wrong economic histories; much of the impossibility literature is based on misunderstanding of the economic history of Africa. The Berge report presented a brief history of Africa's post-colonial development and the state's role in that development. It described both post-colonial policy and performance as absolute and indistinguishable tragedies.

While there were some facts in the report, to a large extent, the report falsified economic performance in the continent. Additionally, the report underestimated the enormous importance of the global influence to Africa; when the world market performs well, African states do well too and vice versa. Moreover, some of the policies followed by African states were formulated by respectable world international institutions, thus making them responsible in bad economic policies, which lead

133

to failure in the continent[40], but the report saddles all blame on Africa (Hofisi, 2013; Mkandawire, 2001).

Furthermore, despite a number of challenges in their economic policies, up until the second "oil" crisis in the late 1970s, some African states had performed comparatively well. Evidence reveals that some countries such as Kenya, Tanzania, Ivory Coast and Malawi had growth rates of more than 6 percent for more than ten years, and this growth was mainly based on agricultural and industrial expansion. An interesting feature here is that much of this growth was sustained principally by local savings. The rates of savings and investments compared relatively well with those of East Asian states, though African savings and investments tended to produce lower growth rates. The states played a central role in the whole planning process and some states such as Ivory Coast and Tanzania were highly interventionist and "dirigiste" with the state

---

[40] This is one of the key points that pushes me to call for African thinking from Africans – unless Africans come up with their own thinking they will continue implementing other people's thinking unsuccessfully. It is difficult to understand fully the thinking of the other, but if one is capable of developing his own why should they rely on the others'. Chapter eight is dedicated for this argument

taking the development role in the agricultural export activities through local parastatals.

Therefore, this proves beyond doubt that Africa has had states whose ideology was clearly "developmentalist" and that they pursued policies that produced fairly high growth rates in the post-colonial era and attained significant social gains and accumulation of human capital. Moreover, some governments extended infrastructure and social services to degrees never thought of under colonial regimes. In addition, many African states were able to maintain peace and security in their countries. Thus, from the arguments above, we realise that "developmental states" are not entirely something new in Africa (Mkandawire, 2001; Sandbrook, 1995).

In response to the impossibility of the developmental states in Africa, Mkandawire (2001) argues that Africa has had developmental states although they were less successful. He argues that Africa can have successful developmental states today. He maintains that the arguments for the impossibility of developmental states

135

in Africa are "not firmly founded either in African historical experiences or in the trajectories of the more successful developmental states" (Mkandawire, 2001 in Hofisi, 2013), hence the call for a developmental orientation of Africa and Tanzania, in particular, which certainly empowers the state not only to formulate policies but also (and more significantly) execute them efficiently and effectively well for the transformation of all people's aspects of life in the country.

Mkandawire's argument sought to respond to critiques who in the 1980s and 1990s argued that African States couldn't become developmental states as did the East Asian states because of weaknesses in African states cultural background, lack of ideology, softness of the African states, lack of technical and analytical capacity, structural reasons and the dependence of rent seeking.[41]This argument serves as well to prepare the mind for the discussion and suggestion put forth in the next chapter. This thinking makes sense as it could be

---

[41]The slogan was coined by Anne Krueger in 1974; she took it from Adam Smith, where originally it meant gaining control of land and or other natural sources. Today it means seeking to increase one's share of existing wealth without creating new wealth. The effects of rent-seeking are reduced economic efficiency through poor allocation of resources, reduced actual wealth creation, lost government revenue, and increased income inequality, and, potentially, national decline.

an alternative development model to address poverty reduction successfully.

Tanzania and the Developmental State

When Tanzania became independent in 1961, it inherited a colonial market economy. The country's economy was performing relatively well, but the benefits of the economy were felt by a small group of individuals, mainly the English and Asian businesses which meant they had the major share of the economy. This market economy was a capitalist model whereby major means of economic production were under the control of the private sector consequently the Tanzanian government did not have authority to intervene even when the market forces failed. Yet the state wanted all citizens to experience economic benefits in a newly independent state (Ngowi, 2009). When it became clearer to the state that it was not possible to realise its development agenda of poverty reduction and bringing equality amongst the people through the same market economy, Ujamaa – a state-led socio, political-economic ideology – was seen as the right strategy to drive and realise the government development agenda (Cornelli, 2012; Kaiser, 1996 in Ngowi 2009).

Under the Ujamaa strategy, the state became responsible in all economic affairs. It became a real developmental state as argues Mkandawire (2001) as it became a "dirigiste economy", planned and "governed the markets" for the purpose of effective accumulation for industrialisation. At this stage, the state became the defender of public order and public property rights responsible of social and physical infrastructure and macro-economic executive. The state assumed as well the roles of economic planning, regulator and to some extent, entrepreneurship, and the private sector disappeared (Sandbrook, 1995).

The scenario in the Ujamaa era had some similarities to what was happening in the 1960s and 1970s in the interventionist policies in the Republic of Korea. However, the Korean developmental state differed from the Tanzanian "developmental state" as the Korea's economic policies relied profoundly on very close consultations between the state and business leaders and very large diversified corporate multinationals (Kasahara, 2013). Since the Tanzanian developmental state under Ujamaa strategy appropriated all the economy and major means of production, and consequently, the disappearance of the private sector, it was not possible to have alternative economic ideas from business leaders in the country. Therefore, the state failed to realise its development agenda, contrary to what happened in the republic of Korea (Tanzania Human Development Report, 2014; Edwards, 2012; Nord et al., 2009; Todaro & Smith 2009).

The failure of Ujamaa as an economic policy led to economic and structural reformation starting in the mid-1980s following fierce pressure from the donor community and the Bretton woods institutions. Thus, Tanzania returned to the market economy which is a neo-liberal approach driven by market forces (Wangwe et al., 2014; Edwards, 2012; Nord et al, 2009). When African states became independent in the early 1960s, Dumont (1966) in Sandbrook (1995) argued that it would have taken two decades for the SSA to kick out poverty completely. However, as argued by Sandbrook

(1995), by 1980s, African states were poor or even poorer than they were twenty years earlier. Borrowing the same argument from Dumont (1966), two decades on since adoption of neo-liberalism in Tanzania, the country has neither become a developmental state nor has it been able to attain its development agenda of poverty reduction. Since independence, Tanzania has experimented both in the state-led economy through Ujamaa (Fouéré, 2014; Edwards, 2012; Nord et al., 2009; Ngowi, 2009; Ibhawoh & Dibua 2003) and the market led economy in this era of neo-liberalism for more than two decades (Tanzania Human Development Report, 2014; Edwards, 2012; Nord et al., 2009).

However, both epochs have failed to bring real substantial progress because despite impressive economic growth in recent years of neo-liberal economy, poverty continues to trouble many Tanzanians, especially the majority of those who live in the rural areas (Tanzania Human Development Report, 2014; Wuyts & Kilama, 2014; Martins, 2013; Mashindano et al., 2013; Mkenda, Luvanda, & Ruhinduka 2010; Policy Forum & Twaweza 2009). At this juncture, it is necessary to rethink a new paradigm – new development philosophy. This study calls for a unification of dependency and neo-liberal thoughts by adopting the Republic of Korea's development model which enabled the republic of Korea become a developmental state and thus industrialise. Tanzania can become a developmental state and hence attain its development agenda by merging the two experiences it has had of state driven and market-led economy.

During the Ujamaa period in 1967– 1985, as discussed earlier, Tanzania adapted the developmental state trajectory as its pathway to development (Kieh-Klay, 2015; Sandbrook, 1995). Therefore, developmental state is not a new concept to Tanzania at all. The question, however, is why did the developmental state in the country fail to become as successful as in the case of South Korea? A number of factors, both internal and external, forced Tanzania to abandon the developmental state (Kieh-klay, 2015). Some of the factors included lack of a vibrant private sector, failure of attracting FDIs, use of obsolete technologies in the industries, and poor economic polies, such as too much

141

state economic intervention which are highlighted in the Mkukuta I strategy (Tanzania Human Development Report, 2014; Ubhenin & Edeh, 2014; Leys, 1996; Sandbrook, 1995).

In this oeuvre we propose developmental state as the appropriate model to attain successfully the country's development agenda and poverty reduction. Tanzania has already experienced the developmental state model. Therefore when it addresses the factors that made it fail to realise its objectives in the first place, it can strive to achieve its plans successfully this time. Moreover, the country has experienced both state-led economy under the influence of dependency school of thought and the open market economy under the influence of neo-liberal policies. Both schools have their strengths and weaknesses as discussed at the beginning of this chapter. These factors have influenced the country's economy accordingly. The study proposes, this time, that Tanzania builds its developmental state model based on the strengths found in the two schools of thought.

In order for Tanzania to become a successful developmental state, there should be a guiding philosophy informing the country. When Tanzania became a developmental state in the period after independence especially from 1967–1985, it was informed by the dependence school. Whereas since mid–1980s to date, it does not have a distinct development model and is being informed by the neo-liberal school. Informed by these facts, the study recommends the use of an amalgamation of revised dependency and neo–liberal schools.

The dependence school calls for revolution and socialism for an economy to industrialise (Siddle & Swindell, 1990). Tanzania employed the dependence ideas through Ujamaa for about twenty years. There were both successes and failures recorded from the school which inform this amalgamation. Socialism in this amalgamation refers to the state that takes the leading role in its economic growth and development without nationalising the major means of production. Economic development will ensure poverty alleviation and thus attain the country's development agenda. By

143

revolution in this aspect, the study refers to the change of a developmental model from the current status of no specific development model to a democratic developmental state.

The neo-liberal school of thought calls for strong reformed institutions, free market and vibrant private sector amongst other factors for an economy to industrialise. Tanzania's economy has, for about thirty years, been informed by neo-liberalism which stirred economic growth. However, neo-liberalism has failed to reduce poverty significantly, especially among the majority rural people because the growth was neither pro-poor nor inclusive (Kessy et al., 2013; Mashindano et al., 2011). Moreover, neo-liberalism operated in an époque where there was no development model in the country. Therefore, in order for economic growth to be inclusive and pro-poor for poverty reduction and attaining the country's development agenda, this study proposes that Tanzania becomes a developmental state while governed by the amalgamation of revised dependency and neo-liberal schools of thought. This model should shift the attention from economic growth, which has failed to reduce poverty significantly, to economic development which adopts new technologies, transiting from an agriculture-based to industry-based economy that improves the standard of living and economic health of a population. The practical aspects of this proposed development model are detailed below in this chapter.

Kieh-Klay (2015), proposes that African countries become developmental states by adhering to important factors that would enable African states become developmental. They include the type of state – the fundaments and development. These factors are the same as those that we in this book argue for and call upon Tanzania to embrace these conditions for a successful developmental state. The factors in the discussion are the same ones in different vocabularies that Kasahara (2013), argued for when explaining the success of South Korea as a developmental state.

However, Kieh-Klay (2015), adds the aspect of democracy as a factor for the same. This is a new factor which adds value to a developmental state and argues for democratic ones contrary to South Korea which was authoritarian but went on to become successful. This is different from Tanzania which was somewhat authoritarian but failed to industrialise. When Tanzania adapts and adopts these factors, then it becomes possible for the country to transform into a successful developmental state this time and thus meet the country's developmental goals and poverty reduction.

Tanzania has favourable conditions for becoming a developmental state as the Republic of Korea had. This is because Tanzania contains some crucial factors and can continue to improve the necessary conditions for converting into a developmental state as long as the political will is there. In East Asia, in general, and in the Republic of Korea in particular, the factors that facilitated the project included good macro-economic management and stability, a competent bureaucracy, interdependence between the public and private sectors, publicly controlled financing for development and industrial policy in a much wider sense (Kasahara, 2013). The factors are summarized into two main ones.

These are competent bureaucracy and embedded economy.

Competent bureaucracy: Amsden (1989) in Kasahara (2013), mantains that competent bureaucracy was one of the necessary factors that made it possible for the developmental state in the Republic of Korea. The country created a pilot agency that was staffed with the country's finest workforce that was given the task of directing the course of the country's development. The pilot agency was empowered with authority to keep on employing outstanding personnel and utilised policy tools to facilitate their work competently. Consequently, the Republic of Korea was able to develop the greatest state capacity both to formulate the right development policies and to execute them efficiently (Kasahara, 2013).

Embedded autonomy: A competent bureaucracy should be able to maintain an effective relationship with the domestic private sector, specifically on the direction and funding in the industrial sector. Evans (1995) in Kasahara (2013), coined the slogan "embedded

147

autonomy" to explain the ideal relationship between the developmental state and the local business sector. He argues that a successful developmental state needs to be sufficiently embedded/rooted in society so as to attain its development agenda by acting through "social infrastructure", but the state should not be too close to the business class to the point of being influenced by particular interests of the private sector and forget its major objective of the development agenda (Kasahara, 2013; Mkandawire, 2001).

Tanzania has necessary conditions for becoming a developmental state and thus attaining its development agenda. The government of Tanzania (2005) acknowledges the importance of the private sector as a key development partner. The government advocates for public, private partnership in the country. This is a good avenue for consultation between the state and the business leaders. Moreover, the country has a strong political will and commitment to continue implementing necessary policy changes and institutional reforms across priority sectors so as to meet the development agenda (USAID, 2014). The political will can facilitate

the formulation of the right policies and implement them
similarly to the Korean model. Tanzania continues to be
a peaceful state – a condition necessary for attraction
of FDI, multinational companies and absorption of
technology and innovation for development, which is
more attainable in developing countries like Tanzania
as such countries need to develop (Kraemer–Mbula &
Wamae, 2010).

Moreover, in order for Tanzania to become successful
in the South Korean way, it is important for Tanzania to
keep health, relationship with the international
community and big world economies including former
colonial masters[42]. Tanzania will have to adhere to the
international programs of global bodies such as the UN
on issues of peace and development, the WB and IMF
on monetary issues and the WTO on fair trade issues.
South Korea, together with all the efforts and hard
work that it put in to build its economy, benefitted so
much in the military aid and trade support from the US

---

[42] While it is important for Tanzania to keep a good diplomatic relation with other
states, it does not mean that Tanzania should not have its own stand on matters
dear to her and her population. On the contrary Tanzania has to redefine and make
clear her national interests and keep them dearly even as it relates with other
states. It should act as a real sovereign conscious of what it is.

and built on as well from the Japanese technology, the former colonial master (Todaro & Smith, 2012; Cha, 2008).

Pragmatic Actions for Developmental State

While in this book we propose that Tanzania becomes a developmental state, this work, informed by findings and analyses of the author from his doctorate research, Mandalu, (2016), has found and affirms that economic growth, which was impressive in the past two or so decades in the country, has failed to reduce poverty significantly amongst the population (Anrdt, 2016; World Bank, 2015; Tanzania Human Development Report, 2014; Kessy et al., 2013, Mashindano et al., 2011; Mkenda et al., 2010; Twaweza, 2009). Therefore, we propose that Tanzania shifts her attention from economic growth, which was one of the major objectives of MKUKUTA I, to economic development[43] which is in line with the objectives of TDV 2025 as it adopts to new technologies, transitions from an agriculture-based to industry-based economy

---

[43] Amartya Sen's (1999) international work considers economic development as the strengthening of autonomy and substantive freedoms, which allow individuals to fully participate in economic life. Hence, economic development occurs when individual agents have the opportunity to develop the capacities that allow them to actively engage and contribute to the economy.

that improves the standard of living and economic health of the people in the country (Feldmanetal, 2014). Cooksey (2013), who in the article "what will it take for Tanzania to become a developmental state?", argues that Tanzania will have to preserve the equilibrium of its economic growth, increase productivity of small holders, improve the quality of its products, efficiency and equity in public goods and social services; channel economic rents into productive activities and create a pro-active industrial strategy that will generate employment opportunities and exports.

What Cooksey (2013) argues about a developmental state in Tanzania is in line with what I in this book and in the thesis propose as the pragmatic interventions of this developmental model. We come up with three practical interventions to implement this proposed development model. The model is expected to enable realisation of the country's development agenda and poverty reduction effectively. The proposed pragmatic interventions are:

1. Strong institutions, the state and the private sector,

2. Rural development and,

3. Education and quality of labour.

Strong Institutions, the State and the Private Sector

For Tanzania to industrialise, it requires a vision that stipulates clearly what it intends to achieve and strategies to implement the vision in terms of poverty reduction and industrialisation. Moreover, the developmental model should consider all hindrances that prevented inclusive economic development to all people during the Ujamaa and in the neo-liberal policies eras. Factors that affected economic development in the country should be well addressed in all productive sectors of agriculture, industry and construction and services. Findings from Mandalu (2016), reveal that Tanzania is well placed to industrialise as the TDV 2025 envisions Tanzania in the category of medium human development by 2025. It is perceived that the country will have transformed from an agricultural society to a semi-industrialised state led by modernized and highly productive agricultural activities linking industrial and services activities in the rural and urban areas. To achieve the development vision, as stipulated in TDV 2025, which is in line with industrialisation; it is then that three factors which are of substantial importance come in. These factors are institutions, the state and the private sector.

1. Institutions

Strong institutions are needed to facilitate professional operation and performance in all productive sectors of agriculture, industry and construction and services for industrialisation to be realised. These institutions will work to make sure that high economic growth is maintained while moving towards economic development which involves all citizens in the country. The country needs to emphasise on the rule of law so that there is transparency and that the checks and balances are observed. There is need for strengthening even more good governance in the country, which will enable the anti-corruption agent fight corruption and address squarely problems arising in the productive sectors such as tax losses due to a number of factors, including corruption in the mining sub-sector, and weaknesses in the tax collection authority.

153

2. The State

The state needs to take an active role in the country's economy becoming a dirigiste state as argued by Sandbrook (1995). It should be able to intervene, show direction and leadership when the market fails to perform properly. The findings in Mandalu (2016) exposed that the government failed to intervene on crops markets in the name of free markets (Mashindano et al., 2013). Moreover, the government should be able to mediate in protecting local industries and businesses so as to empower them to maturity. This is an important practice in the dependence school and should be used to stimulate growth in the domestic industries. Moreover, the government should make sure that the economy becomes inclusive, thus involving and benefiting most or all citizens. This is necessary as the economy should shift the attention from economic growth to economic development (Feldman et al 2014). Furthermore, the state needs patriotic, visionary and indeed ambitious leaders as were the cases in South Korea in 1961-1979 with Park Chung-Hee and Julius Kambarage Nyerere (1922-1999) for Tanzania. Such leaders should be able to give and restore direction of the country's vision when any factors such as unfavourable economic policies or public servants, as was the case of Tanzania during Ujamaa, derail the vision.

3. The Private sector

The country needs to strengthen the private sector as per the study's findings. The sector in Tanzania has been found to be weak and still at infancy stage. Tanzania needs a strong private sector as this is one of the pillars of the neo-liberal policies, and when the sector is strong enough, it employs the largest portion of the labour force, and the sector is a great source of government's revenues. Moreover, the government will have to improve its cooperation with the private sector as the sector should take the leading role of employment generation in the economy. Furthermore, the country needs a strong private sector as this sector would be the source of alternative development ideas to the government, our African countries need locally cultivated ideas. The South Korea government used to consult with the private sector for alternative development thoughts during the industrialisation process (Kasahara, 2013).

Rural Development

Studies have revealed and affirmed that 96 percent of all poor people in the country live in the rural areas, and these people rely on agriculture for their livehoods (NBS, 2014; Mashindano & Maro, 2011). The World Bank report shows that Tanzania has 12 million poor people whereby 10 million of these people live in the rural areas (World Bank, 2015). Thus, if industrialisation and, consequently, poverty reduction are to take place in Tanzania, then rural development through agricultural revolution is inevitable. Rural development can be attained through the following interventions:

1. Improve the agriculture technology currently being used in the agriculture sector in the rural areas, and diversify the quantity of cultivated crops, empower the extension officers through training, and empower them with working tools so that they reach farmers to disseminate the needed technology.

2. Strengthen farmers' cooperative unions and establish them where they do not exist; let the farmers' cooperative unions be empowered and speak for farmers' rights. When cooperative unions are well strengthened they will influence increased productivity.

3. Establish agro-processing industries that will guarantee reliable markets to farmers' crops and also provide employment opportunities in non-farming activities.

4. Improve necessary infrastructure such as road networks, telecommunication (mobile phones) and electricity which will ensure rapid and reliable transportation of agricultural products and exports from agro-processing industries and increase accessibility to other services timeously.

Education and Quality of Labour

The findings observed in Mandalu (2016), have revealed that the population with post-secondary education in Tanzania is minimal when compared to other countries in the development category (Tanzania Human Development Report, 2014). Moreover, findings in the same study have highlighted that the quality of education in the country is poor and thus failing to impart competitive and innovative knowledge and skills to students who are the future labour force. Furthermore, findings revealed that investors had difficulties in finding personnel with competitive skills needed in investors' enterprises. To change the situation and contribute to the country's industrialisation and, subsequently, poverty reduction, the following interventions are essential and necessary:

1. Attract talented students to the education sector and train them to become the best teachers so as to produce brilliant students, and future skilled labour force and job creators. The trained students will be enabled to discover their talents, and thus will be creative, innovative and consequently, in all

productive sectors in the country, there will be needed qualified personnel.

2. Improve the ability and teaching morale of current teachers and future ones by giving them relevant training and providing them with modern teaching tools. Improve their living standards such as the quality of their salaries, houses, health services and provide them with reliable transport where applicable.

3. Improve and build more vocational training colleges and provide mechanisms to change students' mind set and influence more to take science and technical studies. The polytechnic schools will facilitate and ensure creation of innovators and, in the long run, will enable embracing of new technology in all economic sectors of agriculture, industry and construction.

When these pragmatic actions are taken either literary or in another similar form then we strongly believe that the country's economy will change. The real change needs to address the lives of the rural people where poverty is felt through lack of food, shelter and clothing; smelt through poor and bad toilets, and tasted through lack of sugar and salt when meals are secured[44] in everyday life, and in almost every household.

---

[44] Dr. Mwisomba, an expert in economics and statistics, says poverty in Africa can be felt by lack of important needs, tasted by lack of sugar and salt in everyday activities in a household.

CHAPTER EIGHT

THE HIDDEN WEALTH OF TANZANIA

The hidden wealth of Tanzania is deep buried in the corners so unpopular to many Tanzanians. The wealth of the country is not only found in the many and famous tourists' attractions and destinations in the country, but also in other reality of great importance. Some popular tourists destinations in the country include the highest mountain in the continent; Mount Kilimanjaro standing at (5,895 metres above sea level), Lake Tanganyika (358 metres) below sea level; the deepest part of the continent), Serengeti; a great world wonder, Ngorongoro; the crater with amazing features, and Zanzibar; one among the largest islands in the Indian ocean; popular for its amazing traditions and cultures. Moreover, the wealth is found not only in the country's natural resources such as minerals, oil and gas; but also in people.

The real wealth in the country is hidden under the *sea bed* of people's brains. The recapturing of this country's wealth calls for people's intellectual independence. Right now, my take is, most people in the country are operating from other people's dreams, as the most schooled[45] people in Tanzania and in the majority of African countries operate through copied ideas from the western education system. Do not misunderstand me on this matter. It is not about *boko haram*[46]. My argument, understanding and conviction are that every human person is endowned with the potential of great thoughts, and consequently capable of contributing to the world. However, the fact that all people are capable of great thoughts needs to be cultivated, for it is not the case in many African countries. The continent in general and Tanzania in particular need to train their citizens to seek for intellectual independence and contribute fully to the international community according to their inborn capacities. The hidden wealth in Tanzania and in the

---

[45]I prefer using the term schooled as opposed to educated as not all schooled people are necessarily educated.

[46] In Hausa it translates as "Western Education is a sin" accessed on 05/07/2017 at http://www.bbc.com/news/blogs-magazine-monitor-27390954

continent will be rediscovered only when Africans opt for their own cultivated and informed thoughts.

My argument therefore is that the rediscovery of African wealth can be actualised through a non-holy trinity of the study of philosophy, investing in science and technology and practice of African economics.

INTRODUCING PHILOSOPHY TO THE AFRICAN YOUTH

Philosophy is a compound word (Philos-Sophia) meaning the love of wisdom. It is a discipline that trains, empowers, equips and sharpens one's brain so as to search for ultimate truth. Philosophy empowers one to search for the ultimate, the truth as such, the underlying truth of truth itself. The truth in subject could be the truth about almost anything and everything. It equips you with inquisitive mind to search for the truth about all realities such as the world; what is its origin? Can we truly know it as it is? Do we really know things as they are? How do we know that we know?

163

The youth should be taught philosophy because this is the group with the highest number of working individuals as they are neither children nor elders. We expect them to have enjoyed and abandoned their childhood, well armed with parental affection, and that they are now ready to start giving back to society. This is a group of people full of curiosity, inquisitive minds and has many working years ahead for their nation and the human community in general. In Tanzania, young people are termed as individuals aged between 15 and 35[47]. In the same country, a child is considered a person below 18 years of age[48]. If the working age is taken from 18 to 60 years, then that means this young person will have 42 years of service to his country, and thus the need for philosophy training becomes substantiated.

Since philosophy equips an individual to become a truth seeker, then it follows that this individual earns the ability to become a problem solver as well. Problem solving is the major goal of education in the human

---

[47]National Youth Development Policy 2007 at
http://www.youthpolicy.org/national/Tanzania_2007_National_Youth_Policy.pdf
[48]Child Law Act of 2009

society as it enables an individual to dominate his environment; on land, under the waters and in the sky.

The educational objective of problem solving skills can be witnessed through the highest level of education in the world: Doctor of Philosophy (Ph.D). A PhD level of education is meant to providing skills to an individual on how to solve problems facing his community. Therefore, educational institutions and more specifically universities should aim at sharpening scholar's ability in thinking systematically, logically, critically and innovatively. In fact this argument resounds the words of Mwalimu Julius Kambarage Nyerere, who on a university, said any university in the world has the task of training a human person on how to think independently, and acquire skills that enable him become capable of solving problems facing his community.

Moreover, apart from the problem solving skills that the youth should get equipped with; philosophy arms learners with lots of other highly desired skills; knowledge, analysis, critique and qualities that are indeed scarce resources. This section concentrates mainly on freedom, *I-Thou* relation, and happiness.

Freedom

As a philosophy student, I learnt that freedom involves two realities: a subject and an object. Between the two there is a tension or a relationship that is synthesized through the cognitive[49] and affective[50] tension in order to have a good or a decision. All this happens in the will. However, the subject can have a tension either from outside or/and from within itself without necessarily involving the object. In this case we talk of a free will that is movement within the subject. This is what we call freedom. Here the will determines itself and not determined from outside. That is to say, it is auto determined.

However, the freedom referred in this context is about intellectual autonomy. It is true that all human beings are born free[51] and with the most advanced brain

---

[49]The process of knowing / understanding which involves thinking···

[50]That which expresses emotion or feeling; emotional

[51]Article 1 of the Universal declaration of Human Rights declared by the United Nations in 1948

compared to other members in the same animal kingdom. Thus human beings, thanks to their highly developed brain, act intelligently and are capable of higher intellectual activities such as speech, thinking and putting their thoughts in deeds. This is affirmed by scientists that, all human brains have superior brains compared to other animals (Herrmann, et al, 2007). The brain in all human beings has the same essence[52] but with different accidents. The difference in accidents is witnessed by facts and qualities such as time, location, sound and on and on. All human beings are born at different times, location and with different parents[53]; thus the brain acquires different information from different people, culture, experience, different location and on and on. Since knowledge is acquired through senses[54] then the human intelligence gets influenced

---

[52] "Essence" in philosophy is that which makes a being to be what it is... And a "being" is that which is. It is all thanks to Aristotle who made a distinction in the properties of things. The distinction is on essential (essence) and accidental (accidents). For instance, a bed could be wooden or metallic but this is accidental to being a bed; it is still a bed regardless of the nature of the material that is made up of. Aquinas defines an accident in philosophy as that which has its being (existence) in another···

[53] Even children born of the same biological parents; I argue they are still born with different parents in the sense that *you cannot step twice in the same river*. By the time parents give birth to kinds they are always different and that is demonstrated by the genetic makeup of siblings; though born of the same parents; they have some similarities and yet they are different.

[54] Knowledge is acquired through senses thus argue empiricists, and through intellectual a prior thus argue rationalists

through accidents which are necessary to all beings including the human being's brain.

It is thanks to the accidents that people have different thoughts and perception of realities. This difference has misled many respectable thinkers[55] and scientists[56] to think that people of certain races are more intelligent than others. They make such statements without going to the ultimate truth of matters. It is true that some people are more exposed to more facts, experiences and thus appear to be more intelligent than others. The exposures, cultures, and some kind of leadership which empower some individuals to more practical skills influence the individuals to prosper in economic development as compared to those who have not been exposed in the same manner. A case of the Nogales city at the US-Mexican border with people of almost the same settings and cultural backgrounds have

---

[55]Kant, Hegel and other non-African philosophers had very poor notion (racists) on the intellectual ability of African people; of course their claims did not have any philosophical truth and scientific facts. What a shame, heavyweight philosophers with great contribution to humanity allow themselves to become racists.
[56]James Watson, a great scientist, made similar claims about African intelligence too; of course that was refuted and I refute that claim as well. Ben Carson in his *Gifted Hands* said he did not see substantial difference between a black person's brain and that of a white person when he carried out operations to people of all races.

different levels of economic development. Acemoglu & Robinson (2012), argue that the discrepancies in economic development between the two sides of the city are caused by different types of political institutions. My take and common sense are that people with high levels of economic development have put in lots of efforts and discipline in training their brains to acquire the knowledge they possess. I suppose the difference in genetic makeup of human brains contributes in the difference in receptiveness of the brain. And thus there are some people who, influenced by their natural talents and or gifts, dedicate their time and energy in certain fields becoming experts in the discipline. Such thinkers, philosophers, scientists use their talents well for the common good of the human race. Some examples dear to me; Faraday's oeuvre in electricity, Sir Isaac Newton on motion, Thomas of Aquinas on laws, Julius Nyerere on African liberation, Nelson Mandela on South African equality, the list goes on and on.

Most great progress in the human history has been possible; thanks to intellectual freedom. The successful

169

scholars trusted their thoughts and went on to pen them down or to subject them to experiments in the lab or in any other form of testing. Trusting one's intellectual ability and utilizing the intellectual freedom to create constructive and useful ideas lead to great products. People are talented differently hence the need to learn from one another. On learning from others, some may continue with the same thinking while others may emerge with novel thinking. It is all about intellectual freedom and autonomy. To appreciate this theme of intellectual freedom and autonomy I propose our students be taken through a systematic history of philosophy right from the pre-Socratic era to contemporary period.

This experience will take students through different philosophical periods rich in ideas and indeed great thoughts. These periods are ancient Greek era, medieval period, modern era and the contemporary era. This exercise will let them encounter thinkers in logic, epistemology, metaphysics, cosmology, theodicy, and ethics. This experience of taking young scholars through these periods of thinkers will serve them with two purposes.

First, this will help students witness how novel intellectual ideas are shaped by old ones and how the old ones get rejuvenated and carry more significant contribution. Through the periods of time, great world thinkers emerged. Thinkers of all disciplines came from philosophy as philosophy used to house all kind of thinking be it Geography, Astronomy, History, Economics, Laws, Mathematics, Political science, Biology, Physics, Chemistry, Psychology and so on. Thus it is indeed so necessary that young African scholars should go through this "burning furnace".

The second purpose is that all our young Tanzanian or rather, African students will necessary be influenced on how to think systematically, inquisitively and logically. Trust me, they will become thinkers. These new thinkers will come with all sort of useful ideas for the development and wellbeing of our country and the continent. There will emerge patriotic thinkers on different disciplines such as Political science, Political

171

economy, Economics, Political Philosophy, and on and on. The novel patriotic ideas will then be translated into practical disciplines that improve people's living standards including modern housing, health infrastructure, education facilities, accessibility to clean and safe water and making life more meaningful to all justly without treating the other as an object as was the case during slavery and colonialism.

I – Thou Relationship

We live in a capitalistic world that is increasingly becoming globalized[57]. The capitalist world, while being famous for its grand things, is more especially egoistic, and indeed selfish to the point of denying even close relations[58]. In that nature, while it fosters competition for more accumulation of wealth, it does not necessarily

---

[57] In the cold war era (1947-1991) the World was polarised onto the Western and Eastern blocks. The former led by Washington was mainly Capitalistic, and the later led by Moscow was socialists or communist or simply was opposed to capitalism. During the same period, there emerged a group of Non Aligned Movement; states that did not want to subscribe to any of the two blocks. However, with the fall of communism in Russia in 1991, and with the fall of the Berlin war in 1989, the World is fast becoming capitalistic.

[58] On capitalism the aspect of selfishness is expressed through emphasis on individual property rights as argued by several philosophers such as John Locke (1632-1704) and the concept of individual freedom – individualism – is overemphasized beyond the individualism of the enlightened bourgeois liberalism. Margaret Thatcher (the former British Prime Minister), one of the strong proponents of neoliberalism, went even further and claimed that there was "no such thing as society, there are only individual men and women" eventhough she later on accommodated society in the neoliberal project too.

mean success. The capitalist world is ready to treat the other person as an object. The capitalist, while he is enterprising, he cares mostly on profit making before anything else. I know some people will disagree with me on this matter, however we have history to clear any doubts. In slavery and even in colonialism, people were turned into objects and were sold like any other commodities[59]. All that happened in the name of profit making right here on earth.

It is against this background that our Tanzanian, African scholars should not be left to fall deep down into capitalism and forget about human dignity and humanity in general. Capitalists themselves know very well that deep capitalism is not good. You will recall the call for capitalism with a human face[60]. The call for capitalism with a human face justifies that capitalism is an exploitative system of life that degrades the dignity of a

---

[59] Several authors from both the developed and the developing world have attested to this matter. Some references could be useful: Hochschild in King Leopold's Ghost: A story of Greed, Terror and Heroism in Colonial Africa (2006), Acemoglu & Robinson (2012) Why Nations Fail: The Origins of Power, Prosperity and Poverty and Rodney (1972) How Europe Underdeveloped Africa.

[60] Capitalism with human face means what? Does this mean that Capitalism dehumanises a person? If not, why the call for Capitalism with a human face?

human person, and thus the call for personifying it. Hence, I think, this way of life should be replaced.

Gabriel Marcel (1889–1973), a French philosopher, on the above explanation about capitalism, advocated in a way against capitalism that does not value human dignity. He called for the right treatment of a human being because every human person has a dream to fulfill. Marcel takes a human person as a traveller who is always on a journey towards fulfillment. In this journey, a person interacts with fellow human persons who are also searching for means fulfilling their dreams. As they interact, there could be all kind of relations including that of "capitalism" which is profit oriented even to the point of treating a fellow human person as an object. Marcel encourages the treatment of the other as a subject and never as an object since all human beings share human identity and dignity. He coined the term THOU as opposed to IT (Object), thus the relation I – THOU to signify equality amongst human beings. Therefore our call to youth is to learn and internalize the proposed spirit of respect for the other. Thus it is necessary we train our youth to acquire the proposed spirit and be able to cultivate their humane ideologies. We encourage them to absorb the Marcel spirit so that all human beings manage to fulfill their dreams, improve their living standards through the use of local and foreign resources and thus making our people happy and indeed lead a happy life.

Happiness

Aristotle (384-322), one among the great philosophers of ancient Greece, argued that the ultimate purpose of life is happiness. I too affirm and subscribe to that claim and conviction. This statement simply means that whatever activities you carry in life be it business, farming, reading, writing and on and on should aim at making you happy. What makes you happy should make others happy too since most activities involve interaction with your fellow human beings. You have been advised to treat fellow human beings as subjects. That is to say, the preferred relationship should be that of I-THOU. Thus, never deal with your fellow human being as an object. Treating the other as an object or second class human being does not guarantee you true happiness. The aim of life should be the attainment of true and not false happiness. Before embarking into

175

true and false and temporary happiness, we look, briefly though, at what happiness is.

True and false happiness

Happiness is understood differently and by different people through the help of various disciplines. In philosophy, several philosophers, in the course of time, have defined happiness in a number of ways. For Aristotle, happiness is the highest desire and ambition of all human beings which can be attained through virtue[61]. To him, happiness is more of a lifestyle that one experiences through extraction of the best stock of each individual[62]. Jose Ortega Y Gasset (1883–1955), a Spanish philosopher defines happiness as the intersection between projected life and the effective life; that is to say, happiness is attained when what we want to be and what are in reality meet. From the argument, all human beings have the potentiality and desire to become happy. Thus each person defines their reality and what can make them happy.

---

[61]Conformity of one's life and conduct to moral and ethical principles; uprightness; righteousness

[62]Every human person has qualities that can render him/her happy throughout.

And I define happiness as the feeling of satisfaction brought about by fulfillment of one's inner contentment as expressed by tangible basic needs that one has access to or possess. Happiness is the satisfaction with what one has even though it does not limit one from acquiring more so long as amassing of more wealth does not become the driving force of true happiness. In the same line of thought, I categorise happiness on false and true happiness.

True happiness is that which is driven by internal satisfaction, lasts longer, and contains no feelings of guilty as it is obtained through genuine and clean dealings with the OTHER. In a typical capitalistic working world where everybody is busy looking for means of making more money, we take agriculture as an economic activity and source of income from which we extract our example.

> One wealthy farmer, who hires individuals
> and employs machines to work in his field,
> pays workers a wage agreed by both sides.
> In this situation, we take a case of a
> worker who knows very well his rights and
> demands for them. The wealthy farmer,

conscious of injustice done to other workers, makes effort not to be part of the team that pays workers little and dehumanizing wages. Instead he pays a wage acceptable by the highest possible standards of workers' NGOs rights, and well informed workers themselves. When this farmer makes a good harvest he feels happy and satisfied; this happiness is genuine and lasts longer. To me, true happiness, is when two parties in a business are satisfied.

False happiness is that which is propelled by external belongings. This kind of happiness which does not last longer is born in the capitalist system assisted by consumerism behaviour. It is driven by the thirsty for constant wealth accumulation, and in most cases, at any cost.

False happiness is practiced everywhere in the world; while in the developed states it is done through bad contracts, unfair terms of trades which lead in impoverishing the already underdeveloped states. In the underdeveloped states, false happiness is blinding our people as some are busy trying to amass wealth through any possible means; legal or illegal, intelligent or stupid. In Tanzania, Kenya, Malawi and in some other African states, you may recall the search for wealth through superstitious beliefs such as possession of albino body parts would make them rich. Different countries have different superstitious beliefs that would facilitate their becoming rich.

Superstitious beliefs for the purpose of gaining wealth normally lead to bitter results. We have heard of adults doing inhuman acts such as raping kids as young as five, sodomy and the infamous notorious killings of innocent people who suffer from albinism[63]. Such killings were initiated and perpetuated by some witch doctors who cheat[64] people that magic potion mixed with albino body parts would lead to good luck and wealth.

I make it clear that wealth creation is something great and that there is nothing wrong with it. After all wealth was created even before our existence. In fact what we

---

[63]Vick Ntetema http://news.bbc.co.uk/1/hi/world/africa/8674440.stm
http://www.iwmf.org/blog/2010/10/10/vicky-ntetema-2010-courage-in-journalism-award/
[64]They cheat people because superstition is a belief or way of behaving that is based on fear of the unknown and faith in magic – it is a belief that is irrational that which does not involve thinking

179

do is simply wealth accumulation. Wealth accumulation is not bad in itself, for the wealth gathered, when well used serves and saves many lives and purposes. The main issue is on the means and subject of wealth accumulation. The guiding questions here are: What means do you employ to accumulate your wealth? Do you, at any time of your wealth accumulation, exploit a fellow human person? Do you want to amass wealth for the sake of its accumulation, while other human beings die from lack of very basic genuine needs? In such a situation one cannot obtain genuine happiness – I think even sadists may not be happy to witness fellow human beings dying of hunger while they possess a fortune that they, and their children's children, will never be able to use it all. But this is real; we live in the capitalistic world where people die of hunger, while others have more than they can probably be able to consume for the rest of their life. The wisdom of Mahatma Gandhi fits at this junction so well: *"The world has enough resources to satisfy every man's needs, but not enough for every man's greedy wants."* The purpose of this survey in happiness, which is the ultimate purpose of life, is to train our youth to think of others as they think of themselves. We bring it to their conscious right now because through the training in philosophy they become capable of creating their own thoughts which should be mankind conscious.

When our youth are equipped with patriotic and mankind conscious thoughts, then the world becomes a more just and peaceful home for all men and women. People from different continents and countries differ in a number of ways such as religion, skin colour, language, height and on and on. All those differences are accidents that complement a human person. The essence for all human beings is the same to all human beings. The differences in human beings from different places on the face of the world, serve at making the world richer. The variations, which in most cases appear to be talents in human beings, contribute in making the world a much better and interesting place to live in. Our youth should learn that a human person in body and soul needs balanced supplies. The body has its needs which should be supplied and the soul has its own which should be provided too. The provision to body and soul needs to be balanced. Too much supply

181

to the body leads us into consumerism while too much supply to the soul leads us into fundamentalism[65]. In concluding our thinking, philosophy is aimed at empowering our current and future scholars with ideas that are indeed revolutionary for a just world.

The patriotic and mankind conscious thoughts, which are developed through immersion of our youth into philosophy, will be rendered pragmatic through science. Our African countries are obliged to invest in science and technology so that the brilliant developed thoughts get translated into useful means that add value to life through science.

MAKING OUR OWN SCIENTISTS

I propose the transfer and transformation of the developed philosophical thoughts into science, because philosophy is good at digging the deep root of reality of things as they are or as they are supposed to be. While philosophy is good at logical thoughts, science on the other hand, through physical and sensory experiments, transforms ideas/ thinking into pragmatic tangible

---

[65]Rev Dr. Longino Rutagwelera Kamuhabwa: unpublished class notes of Philosophical Anthropology

reality. Both philosophy and science have their strengths and limitations as well, but together they complement each other.

Science is the second stage that you will be exposed to. This follows your philosophical training where your mind will have learnt how to think logically, critically and methodically. Once you graduate in philosophical enquiries which will equip you with useful philosophical thoughts, it is now time to put those philosophical thoughts in the furnace of science where they are transformed into useful products that improve the living standards of people.

Science through inventions, innovation and technologies simplifies enormously the hardship of life while improving the living standard of people. The UN Development agency employs a number of development indicators to measure people's levels of development. Some of the indicators include life expectancy, projected number of schooling years, and income per capita.

Life expectancy is an important indicator which reveals the level of success in healthy facilities in a given country. This indicator is projected from the time when a child is born. The indicator is mainly about advancement in health infrastructure achieved and made available to the population in a given state. Human beings fall sick, what happens when they are ill? Human beings are born fragile and with certain weaknesses in their bodies which calls for improvement in their natural immunity. When you fall sick you do need treatment, you do need specialised health care facilities. When a baby comes into the world it needs immunization so as to boost its levels of immunity. Human beings have been evolving for years and so have their activities and life styles.

The human person, thanks to his thinking and communication abilities, specifically speaking, is always busy conquering his environment. In the course of doing so, he encounters diseases that require his attention. Moreover, human activities and his life style have led to the emergence of all sorts of sicknesses that never existed before and which need the best of his brain's solution for survival. He has to think and find cure for them otherwise he risks extinction. The most natural and advanced instinct of the members of the human race is preservation of their race, hence reproduction for increasing members in the race, and search for cure of maladies to ensure continuity. The cure for diseases threatening man's extinction calls for scientific investigation which results into immunization and cure of the same. In the same efforts to search for cure, dieticians invest time in investigation of the food we eat. Some dieticians through research have affirmed that our eating habits would cure the many ailments that you and I face in life. In these scientific investigations, one observes clearly the collaboration of thinking and pragmatism – philosophy and science. Thus philosophy and science participate in the amelioration of the living standards of a human person. Young African scholars need to search and research in their virgin thoughts so as to contribute more to world civilization through education.

Education is yet another development indicator employed by the UN development agency to measure

185

people's level of human development. Education is a tool for knowledge creation and transitory from one group to another. Education, depending on how it is employed, could be liberating[66] or enslaving. The education we offer to our scholars in Tanzania and Africa in general should identify specific realities found in the country /continent, and should have a direct application that improves his and his community's life. This education that centres on reality found in specific states should, as already presented above, be accompanied with philosophy which helps in doing the magic work of thought provoking and creation which then acts as raw materials for scientific investigation.

According to UN (2009) and Hakikazi (n.d) income poverty is a situation that happens when a household takes in less than one US Dollar per day. This means that persons in the family will not have adequate basic needs. They will not have sufficient food and will have poor clothing and housing. Income poverty is due to

---

[66]An education that empowers an individual by revealing to him/her his/her talents and shows them clearly how they can use them to prosper, improve and contribute to human life is indeed a liberating education. Whereas an education that gives one some tools to work for the other is an enslaving one.

people not having access to money or other assets. If people do not have any other assets like land to grow their own food, then income poverty can result in stunted growth and early death. Income poverty can be reduced and even eradicated by creating more employment opportunities. In Tanzania, economic growth and employment generation is expected from leading economic activities which include, but not limited to, agriculture, manufacturing, service, tourism and mining sectors. While it is necessary for people to work in order for them to earn their income, we propose that people get encouraged to work in the fields that are related to their talents. Moreover, for those who get employed should look for decent jobs.

When people are desperate because of income insufficiency, I know, they will not be choosy about jobs. They will go for anything that generates income to meet their needs. Some employers could also take advantage of the situation, as the International Labour Organisation (ILO) advises, this should respect human rights and dignity. We need not go back to slavery or even in capitalism "with no human face" to re-narrate what happened to human dignity. Those who go for employment should look for decent jobs or rather efforts should be made to make all jobs decent so that human dignity is respected. However, at this section I repeat what I said earlier; young people should be advised to study and work in areas of their talents especially those related to sciences which will eventually stimulate their imagination thus leading to innovation and new technologies.

Innovation and new technologies are results of education and work. Education and work that result into innovation and technology is much wider than schooling in classes and working at a workplace. They involve intellectual ability, readiness and involvement of the body sensory organs. This means seeing, touching, hearing and actual doing. In a nutshell, practice makes it happen correctly. It is this practice that all innovators of all time have employed to benefit our world so that we, who are present today, live more comfortably. You can call to mind a few innovations and discoveries that have forever changed the world and all these and many

more originated in an individual or some individuals'
thoughts.

- The electricity discovery
- The printing press invention
- The floating of objects in water discovery
- The floating of objects in air discovery
- The computers and internet innovation
- The telephone, cell phones, smart phones, smart watches innovation

All these and any other discoveries and inventions may make life much easier or complicated to others. However, the intention of the discoveries and innovations are to add value in life. All inventions have their origin in the human thinking which gets practical input to become what it is today. You see how amazing it is! By being a human person, you are already full of potential in you!

Today most people, worldwide[67], use some kind of modern technology in their daily life. Fortunately and unfortunately[68], in this world of technology there are two relational sides of technology, producers and consumers. Most African countries are mainly consumers of innovation and technological products. I find this situation improper because Africans are human beings capable of thinking and transferring their ideas into pragmatic thoughts which would then be converted to invention and innovation.

A young African scholar should take this challenge seriously. He should not be contented only at having the ability to purchase latest technological devices. An African got to think on how he, through the use of God given talents, could contribute meaningfully to the world. This task is not addressed only to young thinkers – it is addressed to you too even as you read pages of this book. What have you, through your ideas,

---

[67]What tools do the Hadza people in Tanzania use for hunting today?
- http://www.hadzafund.org/Culture.html
- http://www.bbc.com/swahili/habari-40981115 accessed on 24/08/2017
[68]Fortunately there are consumers who will ensure continuity in production and unfortunately as these consumers will be blinded by latest products and fail to discover their potential buried deep down in their brains. This is bad news for the world becomes deprived of new thinking and products from individuals who have failed to check their stock in the store

done to contribute to the improvement of life in your community? How have you helped your children, brothers or sisters to think beyond their surroundings? You should not feel comfortable just because you possess a modern house, a comfortable vehicle, latest version of smart phone, have access to reliable electricity, and are assured of clean and safe water, health food, security and on and on. What actually you should be doing is asking yourself; what is my contribution in making a human life on earth more comfortable and meaningful?

This section calls upon you an African scholar to transfer your novel philosophical thoughts to pragmatic tangible reality. This is the call to you young Tanzanian, young African to rethink of your abilities and see how they would turn you into a scientist who should be able to contribute to your society and the large human community. Staying at the same status of recipient of scientific innovative products from other parts of the planet, you deprive the world of something new and great from you. It is time for Tanzania and Africa to make more scientists who will address our

191

own challenges that are only found in our environment and require specialised knowledge only from our own African scientists. Our science made in the continent need be linked to our own economy by home-made economists for it to be even more meaningful and successful.

MAKING OUR OWN ECONOMISTS

Economics, at its basic nature, is a systematic way of dealing with production, distribution and consumption of goods and services needed by human beings. Moreover, it is a science that includes re-investment of recyclable materials so that the systematic production, distribution and consumption become sustainable.

Economics is a platform for pragmatic philosophy. You may recall pragmatism as a school of thought in philosophy is engaged in that which finds the ultimate truth in ideas that real work, thoughts that produce tangible results. Since it is not possible to lead a meaningful life without economics, then it follows that our young people need the best possible economics education. For the purpose of originality and use of the developed philosophic and scientific thoughts let economics be the right avenue for the practice of those pragmatic thoughts from the learnt philosophy.

As we take the economics field as the practising field of our young people's thoughts, we want them to come up with African economics. We want the young people who will be trained in economics to come up with indigenous economic models. These designed indigenous economic models should use local resources effectively while being environment friendly. The designed indigenous economic models will involve the people, each depending of their specializations, at all levels of production, distribution and consumption in the manner that benefits members of the society. Moreover, in all the processes those economic models should be environmentally conscious. The natural resources available at a given place should not be left at its virgin state[69]. The resources should be used sustainably so that, if possible, it should be allowed to

---

[69]Being left at a virgin state is not acceptable as that will demonstrate inefficiency and weakness of individuals' minds. The virgin resources should be exploited but sustainably for the purpose of meeting needs of people in the society; today and tomorrow.

193

regenerate for use in the future by the coming generations.

The developed local economic models will be designed to be highly productive and effective at meeting the population's needs. Moreover, the models will be designed in such a way that they will be respectful to human dignity and will never, at any point, give importance to profit at the expense of human dignity. No human person should be exploited by economic models in the name of profit making, and out of unhealthy appetites for wealth accumulation.

Political Governing Institutions

As Africa starts using its hidden treasure, the brain reserves which have not been exploited sufficiently. It is necessary to strengthen the state's governing machinery. It is necessary to deal with the governing institution because it deals with who gets what, when and how. Seeing this reality there is need of having fortified institutions that should be able to govern anybody who comes to power. We do not want to experience what happened in the Democratic Republic of Congo (DRC) under Joseph Désiré Mobutu[70]; the country was being governed as a private property stealing and abusing state's resources as the leadership pleased. Mobutu of DRC is not the isolated case that we can learn from. In recent years, some African leaders have been busy influencing their population to change the constitutions or manipulating laws of the land so as to favour their interests. Some countries in the list include Egypt, DRC, Uganda, Rwanda, Burundi, Mali, and Burkina Faso. To make sure the people enjoy the benefits of their land, we reiterate. There is need of having strong governing institutions that would govern and direct anybody who comes to power on how to rule the land without altering the constitution or stealing from the people. The governing institutions should necessarily be in accordance to people's wishes. This

---

[70]In King Leopold's Ghost: A Story of Greed, Terror and Heroism in Colonial Africa; there are tells of how Mobutu treated DRC(then Zaire) as a personal property and on how he stole as much as he could from that resource rich country but with poor population. DRC is great human scandal; the country is a resource rich state but the Congolese are among the poorest people in the world. *King Leopold's Ghost: A Story of Greed, Terror and Heroism in Colonial Africa by Hochschild (2006)* and How Europe Underdeveloped Africa by Rodney (1972) reveal how 'developed states' stole and steal resources from resource rich but underdeveloped states. Even before Mobutu came to power, the author reveals to us how unfair trades were being carried out in the DRC from Africa the ships went to Brussels with ivory, diamond and all kind of riches where as to Africa (DRC) the ship went with gunpowder···

matter calls to mind the social contract theory.[71] This contract though was put forth by western philosophers. It is universal and thus applicable to all human races.

Our philosophers, scientists and economists who dedicate their time and energy for rigorous training for the purpose of serving their country should be protected and led by intelligent politicians. At times, there could be selfish, poorly trained politicians leading our countries. The poorly trained wealth greedy and selfish politicians at times frustrate educated, patriotic and talented technocrats. These well trained professionals need patriotic and good leaders to govern them for greater efficiency and economic development in the country. Good leadership is a desire of people of all walks of life; however, the media, as a component of the population, has a special responsibility on the same, and on encouraging the youth to explore their talents.

---

[71]Jean Jacques Rousseau, Thomas Hobbes, and John Locke, are among the first philosophers who engaged their thoughts on Social Contract. The Social Contract is an agreement made between politicians and the citizens. They enter into a contract where by politicians are supposed to serve for the interests of those who elected them. This contract is guided and operates through a constitution that is made by the people or through their representatives. The contract should be held dearly and that leaders who fail to serve the people's interest according to the interest should be ready to resign

The Media's Role on the Hidden Wealth

The media has a great role to play in a country. If well used it can help spread the development agenda, whereas if it is abused it can lead to catastrophic consequences as the case of *Radio Mille Collines* in Rwanda in 1994. On our agenda, the media houses have a great role on sensitizing people and young people in particular so as to encourage them to extract their talents for self-development and for the development of their country. Most radio stations and newspapers have common and ordinary programs and themes. They lack critical programs that would trigger individuals to reflect on their lives as Socrates once said: *"an unexamined life is not worth living"*. Most radio stations are busy advertising products made overseas, and have ordinary programs mostly on leisure that do not necessarily activate the brains of our youth to think critically and thus emerge with pragmatic solution to society's problems.

REFERENCES

Acemoglu, D & Robinson, J.A,. 2012. Why Nations Fail: The Origins of Power, Prosperity and Poverty. Crown Publishers, New York

Arndt, C., Demry, L., McKay, A. & Tarp, F. 2016. Growth and Poverty Reduction in Tanzania, in *Growth and Poverty in Sub-Saharan Africa*, Arndt, C., McKay, A. & Tarp, F (Eds), UNU-WIDER, New York: Oxford University Press.

Balozi, M.A., Othman.S.Z. & Issa, F.M. 2014. Constructing Theory with Big Result Now: Contribution of Tanzania to the Theory of Knowledge Sharing Behaviour. *International Journal for Innovation Education Research, 2-8.*

Boesen. J., Madsen, B.S. & Moody, T. 1977. *Ujamaa-Socialism from Above.*
Uppsala: Scandinavian Institute of African Studies.

Cha, M. 2008. The Economic History of Korea. EH.Net Encyclopedia, edited by Robert Whaples. Retrieved on 07 August 2016 at http://eh.net/encyclopedia/the-economic-history-of-korea/

Chaibong, H. 2008. South Korea's Miraculous Democracy. Journal of Democracy, Volume 19. Number 3

Chu, J. 2009. Rwanda Rising: A new model of Economic Development, Fast Company Newsletter access on 04/07/2017 at https://www.fastcompany.com/1208900/rwanda-rising-new-model-economic-development

Cooksey, B. 2013. 'What will it take for Tanzania to become a developmental state? Evidence from Tanzania Governance

Review 2010-11. *Policy Forum Breakfast Debate* 22 February, Dar es Salaam.

Cornelli, M.E. 2012. A critical Analysis of Nyerere's Ujamaa: An investigation of its foundations and values. PhD dissertation, *University of Birmingham.* Accessed on 26th June 2014 at:
http://ethese.bham.ac.uk/3793/1/Cornelli_12_PhD.pdf

Corta, L. & Magongo, J. 2010. Evolution of Gender and Poverty Dynamics in Tanzania', *Chronic Poverty Research Centre, Working Paper.* Accessed on 1st April 2015 at http://www.chronicpoverty.org/uploads/publication_files/da-corta-magongo.pdf

Coulson, A. 2014. Conference of 50 years of Development in Sub Saharan Africa: The experience of Tanzania, Bradford University, England 29-30 May Accessed 07th November 2015 at
http://www.bradford.ac.uk/socialsciences/media/ssis/bcid/ta
nzaniaconference2014papers/Coulson-From-the-Arusha-Declaration-to-Big-Results-Now-The-Political-Economy-of-Tanzania.pdf

Crisafulli, P. & Redmond, A. 2012. The Rwanda Model: Focus on Poverty, entrepreneurship, Human Capital, Institutions, and accountability, American Outlook accessed on 04/07/2017 at
http://www.americanoutlook.org/rwanda-model.html

Daima Associates Limited. 2007. Opportunities and Risks of Liberalizing Trade in Services in Tanzania. *International Centre for Trade and Sustainable Development*, Issue Paper No.4.

Edwards, S. 2012. Is Tanzania a success Story? A long term Analysis. *National Bureau of Economic Research,* working paper 17764.

Feldman, M., Hadjimichael, T., Kemeny, T & Lanahan, L. 2014. Economic Development: a definition and model for investment. Accessed on 26th April 2015 at https://www.eda.gov/tools/files/research-reports/investment definition-model.pdf

Frank, G.A. 1969. Latin America: Under-development or Revolution. *New York Monthly Review Press.*

Fouéré, M. 2014. Julius Nyerere, Ujamaa, and Political Morality in Contemporary Tanzania. *African Studies Review, 57(1):1-24.*

Green, M. 2013a. *Understanding the Process of Economic Change:Technology and Opportunity in Rural Tanzania,* Special Paper 13/1, Dar es Salaam, REPOA.

Green, M. 2013b. *Evidence, Economics and Exclusion: Super Actors, Civil Society and Citizen debate in the post MDG paradigm,* Briefing Paper, International NGO Training and Research Centre.

Hakikazi. n.d. Types of Poverty. Accessed on 17th May 2015 at http://www.hakikazi.org/zwp/types_of_poverty.htm.

Hansen, A. 2010. Integration and Late Industrialisation: The Effects of Neoliberal Economic Globalisation on Development and Late Industrialisation. *esharp, issue 15: Uniting Nations: Risks and Opportutie*s.

Harvey, D. 2005. *A Brief History of Neoliberalism.* Oxford: Oxford University Press.

Herrmann, E., Call, Josep., Victoria Hernandez-Lloreda, M., Hare, B., & Tomasello, M. 2007. Humans Have Evolved Specialized Skills of Social Cognition: The Cultural Intelligence Hypothesis, Science, Vol. 317, Issue 5843, pp.1360-1366 DOI: 10.1126/science.1146282 accessed at http://science.sciencemag.org/content/317/5843/1360.full

Heywood, L. 2013. Why Did South Korea Grow Rich, 1960-1985? E-international Relations Students. Accessed 26th March 2016 at http://www.e-ir.info/2013/03/16/why-did-south-korea-grow-rich-c-1960-1985/

Higgins, K. 2013. Escaping Poverty in Tanzania: What Can We Learn From Cases of Success?' in Kessy et al. 2013, *Translating Growth into Poverty Reduction: Beyond the Numbers*, Dar es Salaam: Mkuki na Nyota.

Hochschild. A. 2006. King Leopold's Ghost: A Story of Greed, Terror and Heroism in Colonial Africa, Macmillan, London

Hofisi. C. 2013. "After the Lost Decades: Rethinking Africa's development from a Development State perspective," *Mediterranean Journal of Social Sciences, Rome: MCSER Publishing, Vol.4 No.11 October.*

Holik, J. 2011. Malaysia: Between Democracy and Authoritarianism. Association for International Affairs. Research Paper 5

Human Development Report, 2015. *Work for Human Development*, New York: United Nations Development Program

Human Development Report. 2014. *Human Progress: Reducing Vulnerability and Building Resilience.* New York: United Nations Development Program.

Human Development Report. 2010. *The Real Wealth of Nations: Pathways to Human Development.* New York: United Nations Development Program.

Human Rights Watch World report 2017, Rwanda events of 2016. Accessed on 21st July 2017 at https://www.hrw.org/world-report/2017/country-chapters/rwanda

Ibbott, R. 2014. *Ujamaa: The hidden Story of Tanzania's socialist villages*, London: Cross Roads Books.

Ibhawoh, B. & Dibua, I.J. 2003. Deconstructing Ujamaa: The legacy of Julius Nyerere in the quest for Social and Economic Development in Africa. *African Journal of Political Science, 8(1)*

ILO (International Labour Organisation). 2014. World of work report 2014: Developing with Jobs. Geneva. ILO.

IMF. 1969. Survey of African Economies. Washington DC: *IMF.*

Jerven, M. 2014. African Growth Miracle or statistical tragedy: Interpreting trends in the data over the past two decades. *Wider Working Paper No.114, UNU-WIDER.*

Jules, D.T. (n.d). The Poverty Reduction Strategy Paper and Tanzania's Next Generation. *Journal of education*, Columbia University, Accessed on 2nd June 2015 at *http://www.tc.columbia.edu/sie/journal/Volume_4/Jules_Web site%20Final.pdf.*

Johnson, R.W. 2000. Nyerere: A Flawed Hero. *The National Interest, Washington DC, Vol.60.*

Kaijage, F. & Tibaijuka, A. 1996. Poverty and Social Exclusion in Tanzania. Research Series, Geneva: ILO.

Kaiser, P.J. 1996. Structural Adjustment and the Fragile Nation: The demise of social Unity in Tanzania, *Journal of Modern African Studies 34(2): 227-237.*

Kasahara, S. 2013. The Asian Developmental State and the Flying Geese Paradigm. *United Nations,* United Nations Conference on Trade and Development, Discussion Papers No.213.

Kieh-Klay, G. 2015. Constructing the Social democratic developmental state in Africa: lessons from the Global South. *Journal of the Global South: a Springer Open Journal.*

Kim, S.K., 1991. The Korean Miracle (1962- 1980) revised: Myths and Realities in strategy and development. Working paper No.166 November, the Helen Kellogg Institute for International studies

Korea.net: the Gateway to Korea. n.d. The Korean Economy-the Miracle on the Hangang River. Accessed on 22nd July 2017 at http://www.korea.net/AboutKorea/Economy/The-Miracle-on-The-Hangang

Kraemer-Mbula, E. & Wamae, W. 2010. The Relevance of Innovation Systems to Developing Countries,' in *Innovation and the Development Agenda,* eds Kraemer-Mbula, E & Wamae, W. OECD/IDRC: OECD Publications.

Krueger, A. 1990. Government Failures in Development. *Journal of Economic Perspectives, 4(3). 9-23.*

Landau, L. 1998. National Politics in Post-Nyerere Tanzania? Political Implications of the 1995 Multiparty Elections.*Ufahamu, Vol.XXVI, No.1.*

Lewis, A.W. 1954. Economic Development with unlimited Supplies of Labour. *The ManchesterSchool, 22 (2):139-191.*

Leys, C. 1996. *The rise and fall of Development Theory.* Nairobi: East African Educational Publishers.

Mandalu, M.P, 2016. Tanzania's Development Agenda and Poverty Reduction: A Case of MKUKUTA I, PhD Thesis, University of Fort Hare

Martins, P. 2013. *Growth, Employment and Poverty in Africa: Tales of Lions and Cheetahs.* Overseas Development Institute·Background paper for the World Development Report.

Mashindano, O., Kayunze, K., Corta, L & Maro, F. 2013. Growth Without Poverty Reduction in Tanzania—Reasons for the Mismatch' in Kessy et al. *Translating Growth into Poverty Reduction: Beyond the Numbers,* Dar es Salaam: Mkuki na Nyota.

Mashindano, O. & Maro, F. 2011. Growth without poverty reduction in Tanzania: Reasons for the Mismatch', Working Paper No.207, *Chronic Poverty Research Centre*

Mashindano, O., Kayunze, K., Corta, L. & Maro, F. 2011. 'Agricultural Growth and Poverty Reduction in Tanzania 2000-2010: Where has Agriculture worked for the poor and what can we learn from this? Working Paper No.208, *Chronic Poverty Research Centre*

Mayasian government.2016. The Malysian Economy in Figures. Economic Planning Unit, Prime Minister's Department accessed on 21st July 2017 at http://maddruid.com/wp/wp-content/uploads/2017/03/MEIF-2016.pdf

McMillan, M. & Harttgen, K. 2014. *What is driving the African growth miracle?* National Bureau of Economic Research, Working paper 2007.

Mhando, L. 2011. Tanzania and the Geo-politics of Rural Development: The return of Neoliberalism. *Journal of Emerging Knowledge on Emerging Markets, 3*

Mirambo:

-https://afrolegends.com/2014/05/05/mirambo-the-black-napoleon/ Accessed 08/08/2017
-http://www.blackpast.org/gah/mirambo-ca-1840-1884 Accessed on 09/08/2017
-https://www.britannica.com/biography/Mirambo Accessed on 08/08/2017
-https://www.jamiiforums.com/threads/mirambo-the-man-who-changed-the-face-of-nineteenth-century-tanzania.424773/ Accessed on 09/08/2017

Mkandawire, T. 2001. Thinking about developmental States in Africa. *Cambridge Journal of Economics, 25, 3*

Mkenda, A.F., Luvanda, E.G. & Ruhinduka, R. 2010. *Growth and distribution in Tanzania: Recent experience and lessons.* Dar es Salaaam: *Repoa.*

Msambichaka, L., Luvanda, E., Mashindano, O. & Ruhinduka, R. 2010. Analysis of the Performance of Agriculture Sector and its Contribution to Economic Growth and Poverty

Reduction. *Ministry of Finance and Economic Affairs in Tanzania.*

Moreira, B.S. & Crespo, N. 2012. *Development Economics from the traditional approaches to the New concepts: New Challenges of Economic and Business Development.* Latvia: University of Latvia.

Msola, P. 2008. *Priorities of the national strategy and the millennium Development Goals in Achieving Sustainable Development and Promoting Development Cooperation.* New York: United Nations.

Muganda, A. 2004. Tanzania's Economic Reforms and Lessons learned, Scaling up poverty Reduction. *A global Learning Process and conference Shanghai, May 25-27, 2004.*

National Bureau of Statistics. 2014. Formal Sector Employment and Earnings Survey 2013. Dar es Salaam: Ministry Finance.

National Bureau of Statistics (NBS). 2014. Statistical Abstract 2013. Dar es Salaam: Ministry of Finance.

Ngowi, P.H. 2009. Economic Development and change in Tanzania since independence: The Political leadership factor. *African Journal of Political Science and International Relations 3(4):259-267.*

Nord, R., Sobolev, Y., Dunn, D., Hajdenberg, A., Hobdari, N., Maziad, S. & Roudet, S. 2009. Tanzania: The Story of an African Transition. Washington, D.C: *International Monetary Fund.*

Nursey-Bray, P.F. 1980. Tanzania: The Development Debate. *African Affairs,* 79.

Nyerere, J.K. 1961. *Scramble for Africa: Address to the World Assembly of Youth*. Dar es Salaam: Government Printer.

Nyerere, J.K. 1977. *Ujamaa: Essays on Socialism*. Dar es Salaam: Oxford University Press.

Oberdaberning, D.A. 2010. *The effects of Structural AdjustmentPrograms on Poverty and Income Distribution*. University of Innsbruck Retrieved at
Accessed on 1st June 2015 at:
http://economics.soc.uoc.gr/macro/docs/Year/2011/papers/paper_2_114.pdf

Osafo-Kwaako, P. 2011. *Long-run Effects of Villagization in Tanzania*. Northeast Universities Development Consortium Conference.

Policy Forum & Twaweza. 2009. *Growth in Tanzania: is it Reducing Poverty?* Accessed on 11th November 2014 at:
http://www.twaweza.org/uploads/files/Groth%20in%20Tanzania_Policy%20Forum.pdf

Pratt, C. 1976. *The Critical phases in Tanzania 1945-1968: Nyerere and the emergence of Socialist strategy*, Cambridge: Cambridge University Press.
Research and Analysis Working Group. 2009. Poverty and Human Development Report. Dar es Salaam: REPOA.

Research and Analysis Working Group. 2011. Poverty and Human Development Report. Dar es Salaam: REPOA.

Rodney, W. 1973. *How Europe Underdeveloped Africa*. Dar es Salaam: Tanzania Publishing House.

Rydenfelt, S. 1986. *Lessons from Socialist Tanzania.*
Retrieved at http://www.fee.org/the_freeman/detail/lessons-
from-socialist-tanzania On 25 June 2014.

Sandbrook, R. 1995. *The Politics of Africa's economy
recovery.* Cambridge: Cambridge University Press.

Sansa, G. 2010. 'The Impact of Institutional Reforms on
Poverty and inequality in Tanzania,' PhD Thesis, *University
of Bath* Accessed on 26th May 2015 at:
http://opus.bath.ac.uk/25426/1/UnivBath_PhD_2010_G_Sansa
.pdf.

Scott, J.C. 1999. *Seeing Like a state: How Certain schemes
to Improve the Human Condition have failed.* New Haven:
Yale University Press.

Scott, R.B. 2006. *The Political Economy of Capitalism,*
Working Paper No.07/037, Harvard Business School,
Accessed on 05th November 2015 at
http://www.hbs.edu/faculty/Publication%20Files/07-037.pdf

Seidman, A. 1972. *Comparative Development Strategies in
East Africa.* Nairobi: East Africa Publishing House.

Shivji, I.G. 2008. *Accumulation in an African periphery: A
Theoretical Framework,* Presentation at the 13th REPOA
Research workshop, Dar es Salaam.

Shivji, I.G. 1974. *The silent class struggle,* Dar es Salaam:
Tanzania Publishing House.

Siddle, D. & Swindell, K. 1990. *Rural Change in Tropical
Africa From Colonies to Nation- States.* Oxford: Basil
Blackwell.

Skinner, G. 2011. The Neoclassical Counterrevolution and Developing Economies: A Case Study of Political and Economic Changes in the Philippines. *Social Sciences Journal, 7(1): 12.*

Tanzania Human Development Report. 2014. *Economic Transformation for Human Development.* Dar es Salaam: Economic and Social Research Foundation.

Todaro, M.P. & Smith, S.C. 2009. *Economic Development.* Boston: Pearson Addison Wesley.

Todaro, M.P. & Smith, S.C. 2012. *Economic Development* (11th ed.). Boston: Pearson Addison Wesley.

Ubhenin, O.E. & Edeh, N.J. 2014. Asian Developmental states: Lessons for Africa. *YonetimBilimleri Dergisi, 12(1):7-42.*

UNDP. 2011. International Human Development Indicators, retrieved from
http://hdr.undp.org/en/statistics/ on 26th January, 2012.

UNIDO (United Nations Industrial Development Organisation). 2013. *Industrial Development Report 2013, sustaining Employment Growth: The Role of Manufacturing and structural change.* Geneva: *UNIDO.*

United Nations (UN). 2014. *Economic Development in Africa: Catalysing investment for transformative Growth in Africa,* Conference on Trade and Development.

UN. 2003. *Monterrey Consensus on Financing for Development.* United Nations, International Conference on Financing Development, Monterrey, Mexico 18 – 22 March 2002

UN. 2007. *The United Nations Development Agenda: Development for All*. New York: UN Publications.

UN. 2009. *Rethinking Poverty, Report on the World Social situation 2010, Department of Economic and Social Affairs*. New York: United Nations Publication. Accessed on 6[th]July 2015 at http://www.un.org/esa/socdev/rwss/docs/2010/fullreport.pdf

UN. 2012. *Global profile of Extreme Poverty. Background paper for the High-level Panel of Eminent Persons on the post 2015 Development Agenda. Sustainable Development Solutions Network*. Accessed on 26th April 2015 at http://unsdsn.org/wp-content/uploads/2014/02/121015-Profile-of-Extreme-Poverty.pdf

United Republic of Tanzania. 1999. *Tanzania Development Vision 2025*, Dar es Salaam: Ministry of Planning.

United Republic of Tanzania. 2005. *National Strategy for Growth and Reduction of Poverty*, Dar es Salaam: Vice President's Office.

United Republic of Tanzania. 2010. *National Strategy for Growth and Reduction of Poverty II*. Dar es Salaam: Ministry of Finance and Economic Affairs.

United Republic of Tanzania. 2011a. *Review of the Tanzania Development Vision 2025, Volume I: Main Report*. Dar es Salaam.

United Republic of Tanzania. 2011b. *Accelerating Progress Toward the MDGs Addressing Poverty and Hunger*. Dar es Salaam.

United Republic of Tanzania. 2012. *The Tanzania Five Year Development Plan 2011/12 – 2015/16: Unleashing*

Tanzania's Latent Growth Potentials. Dar es Salaam: President's Office, Planning Commission.

United Republic of Tanzania. 2014. *Education for All National Review.* Dar es Salaam: Ministry of Education and Vocational Training.

United Republic of Tanzania. 2014. *Tanzania Human Development Report 2014: Economic Transformation for Human Development.* Dar es Salaam: Ministry of Finance.

USAID. 2014. Country Development Cooperation Strategy October 3, 2014 – October 3, 2019: Tanzania's Socio-Economic Transformation toward Middle Income Status by 2025 Advanced.

Yusof, Z.A. & Bhattasali, D. 2008. Economic Growth and Development in Malaysia: Policy Making and Leadership. *World Bank,* Commision on Growth and Development, Working paper No.27.

Wangwe, S., Mmari, D., Aikaeli, J., Rutatina, N., Mboghoima, T. & Kinyondo, A. 2014. The Performance of the Manufacturing Sector in Tanzania: Challenges and the way forward. *Wider Working Paper 2014/085.*

Wangwe, S. & Charle, P. 2005. *Macro-economic Policy choices for Growth and Poverty Reduction: The Case of Tanzania.* Dar es Salaam: Economic and Social Research Foundation.

Wobst, P. 2001. *Structural Adjustment and Intersectoral Shifts in Tanzania: A Computable General Equilibrium Analysis.* Research Report 117, International Food Policy Research Institute, DC.

World Bank. 2015. *Tanzania Mainland Poverty Assessment.* Washington DC: World Bank.

World Bank. 2015. *Global Monitoring Report 2014/2015: Ending Poverty and Sharing Prosperity.* Washington, DC: *World Bank.*

Wuyts, M. & Kilama, B. 2014. The Changing Economy of Tanzania: Patterns of Accumulation and structural change. Dar es Salaam: *ESRF and REPOA.*